STUDENT HEALTH

Ever-rising academic standards place a severe strain on student health. Indeed, Modern A-level qualifications would have earned a degree a decade or so ago. There is evidence of worried students being driven to the point of suicide in the rat-race for higher qualifications; among schoolchildren, too, drug overdoses may result from the unremitting pressures to cope with examinations.

Dr. Cauthery is an experienced University student health doctor. He offers tutors and health counsellors a blueprint for better student health by providing them with a deeper knowledge of the causes of excessive strain, and early recognition of its symptoms. The book constitutes a sympathetic guide to the treatment and prevention of students' emotional, sexual, psychiatric and work-stress problems. This is a timely educational handbook, useful not only to doctors and nurses already working in this branch of medicine, but to those entering this important field for the first time.

THE CARE AND WELFARE LIBRARY

Consultant Medical Editor: Alexander R. K. Mitchell, MB,
ch.B, MRCPE, MRCPsych.

STUDENT
HEALTH

PHILIP CAUTHERY
MB, ch.B, DPH
University Physician, The University of Aston in Birmingham

Foreword by
NICOLAS MALLESON MD, MRCP
Director, Research Unit for Student Problems,
University of London

PRIORY PRESS LIMITED

The Care and Welfare Library

SBN 85078 059 4 (Paperback)
    85078 058 6 (Hardback)
Copyright © 1973 by Philip Cauthery
First published in 1973 by
Priory Press Limited
101 Grays Inn Road London WC1
Made and printed in Great Britain by
The Garden City Press Limited
Letchworth, Hertfordshire SG6 1JS

Contents

Contents

Foreword

by Nicolas Malleson MD, MRCP

FOR the last seven years Dr. Philip Cauthery has been one of my closest colleagues. It was with great pleasure that I learnt he was writing a book outlining the problems of student health work for the intelligent lay reader. There is a great need to increase understanding amongst students, their families and among large numbers of staff in higher and further education as to the nature of student distress and what we can or cannot manage to do to be helpful, for the whole subject is one of rapidly growing importance.

As far as the U.K. goes, as a recognizable undertaking Student Health began soon after the war. Nearly all doctors with a serious involvement in the work are members of the British Student Health Association, and the individual medical membership in 1971 was four times the membership in 1960. Perhaps the most striking thing in the picture at present is that student health activity is virtually confined to the university sector. Yet there are nearly as many students in full-time teacher training or degree and diploma level work in the public sector as there are in the universities (207,000 vs. 220,000, approximate figures 1969/70). The projections for 1981 suggest perhaps 370,000 for the public sector, and 460,000 for the universities, a total full-time student population of 830,000. It is clear that the public sector and the Polytechnic in particular, represents an undeveloped growth point in student health work comparable to that of the universities in the beginning of the 1950s.

The Royal College of Physicians report on student health services dated 1966 suggested that one student health physician (or two half-timers) per 2,000 students was a reasonable staffing objective. This appears to be about the present situation—eighty full-timers and eighty part-timers serving 220,000 university students with their concomitant duties for the staff. If today the public sector were providing student health services on the same scale the number of student health doctors would be nearly doubled. By 1981 such a provision may be effectively made, in which case with the expanding student numbers, we may expect some 350 full-time physicians and, say 550 part-timers. Many of the public sector colleges, colleges of education in particular, are small institutions which will be better served by the part-time workers. One might also consider the growing trend for student health services, in appropriate circumstances, to care for the young hospital nurse of which there are perhaps 85,000. For comparison's sake, there are some 320 consultant paediatricians employed by the National Health Service. In short within a decade or two we will be looking at a professional group of nearly 1,000 doctors engaged full-time or part-time in student health work, and it is certainly legitimate to look upon student health work as an established career speciality which one way or another will care for a million people, that is two per cent of our population, and will involve some one per cent of all U.K. doctors.

It is difficult to be precise about the range of interest and background of doctors in student health work, but projecting in a rather loose away from the present situation to 1981 one might expect some 350 part-time G.P.s with specifically student health service commitment, some 200 psychiatrists each doing several sessions in student health work, with a core of 350 full-time student health physicians in career posts.

What can be said about the job specifications for the full-time student health physician, those of us who necessarily make the core of the speciality?

(*a*) by and large, save for an occasional clinical assistantship, we do not work in hospitals.

(*b*) We usually do some general practice, usually holding a N.H.S. list and the work we do in this context is of the highest standard of Out-Patient Department care normally with all special investigation facilities readily available to us ... we are, that is to say, fully competent physicians on the organic side as far as our age group at risk is concerned.

(*c*) We are all in varying degrees psychiatrically sophisticated and a good deal of our time is spent on the psychiatric side of the work, albeit our psychiatric skills and training are usually limited to those relevant to the student age group and to the high grade quality of our population at risk. Our particular skills are in supportive care, in psychodiagnosis, and, to varying extent, in a long-term dynamic psychotherapy for intelligent well-motivated neurotic subjects.

(*d*) We are occupational health advisers advising our institutions on the working conditions of our patients. In this sense we are even more occupationally involved than the ordinary factory doctor in that the 'patient' is also the 'product' of the productive process which employs us.

(*e*) We are health educators. I do not mean by this that we give formal lectures in health education—not many of us do. But we educate our individual patients in their own care and their own medical problems by virtue of having time for thoughtful work and ample discussion with our intelligent clientele. Even more than this, however, the quality of our services set up a level of expectation for health care with the ten per cent elite of the population. This elite, in due course, will exercise consistent pressure upon the National Health Service and ancillary welfare services to achieve comparable standards.

In student health service work we have followed behind the U.S.A. with some time lag, but we can benefit from their experience. In the typical American student health centre there is an organic department and a separate psychiatric or mental hygiene department on a different floor or in a different building. Typically the British student health physician feels competent in both and carries the organic and the psychiatric side of medical work for his particular population. I think we may say that student health—even a bit more than paediatrics—is one of the few areas in which a doctor has an opportunity to be fully competent across the body/mind schism which so regretfully splits many medical services of the Western world. We also have opportunities for avoiding the schism between the psychiatrist in the medical context and the lay student counsellor working either with that title, or with other titles, in a diversity of different pastoral agencies within the college. It is inevitable with the growing student population and with an increasingly high expectation of standards that personal problems cannot only be met by doctors. Logistically it is not possible. In my view it is not even desirable. Ideally educational institutions should have as many agencies—by which I mean people—to whom the troubled students can turn. There should be other doors beyond the medical door through which he can enter care. What matters is that there is a wide corridor connecting those doors.

Many student health centres employ non-medical personnel in this field. Because they work in a medical setting it seems appropriate to call what they do psychotherapy. The same sort of work using the same sort of skill and training but not in a medical setting is properly called counselling. Student counsellors may work under that title with direct self-referral access from the students, or they may work with appointment officers, chaplaincies, etc., or in varying forms of tutorial capacity. It seems to me very important that student health physicians maintain the very warmest links with what is clearly going to be a growing profession, eventually perhaps numerically no smaller than our own. An Association of Student Counsellors has recently been formed and should have every encouragement from the doctors.

The student health service should in the first place be able to cope with most student neurotic disturbances. Although a proportion of them may present directly as, for example, examination anxiety, others may masquerade as minor physical illnesses. Some of the more serious personality disorders and the frank psychotic illness cases will need the help of the local mental health services. Although the number of student cases referred is a small proportion of the case load of the psychiatric service such cases are commonly very time consuming and usually need to be seen swiftly. In consequence additional senior psychiatric sessions are likely to be necessary in university and college towns and one is pleased to note that the Regional Hospital Boards in some areas have provided psychiatric consultant facilities specifically to deal with student cases. It needs to be emphasized that a psychiatrist who regularly sees student cases must have a special knowledge of and interest in the psychiatry of young adults and, equally important, familiarity with the life and organization of the local educational institutions to which the students belong.

Of course, the professional student health and counselling services do not have a monopoly in helping students with psychological disturbances. There are other traditional and valuable sources of help, for example, chaplains, tutors, hostel wardens, lodging officers, and so on. A close liaison between them and the professional services is essential, and the training of our colleagues in the recognition of psychological disturbances and their proper handling either by themselves or by referral is an important aspect of the work of the student health service.

Dr. Cauthery's appraisal and presentation of the whole range of student problems seems to me to have got the balance right and it is a pleasure to introduce this book.

Nicolas Malleson, MD, MRCP

London, 1973.

Preface

I HAVE tried in this book to portray the range and scope of contemporary medical care of the student. A student is here defined as an individual who systematically follows a course of formal academic study, the successful conclusion of which is marked by the issue of some form of recognized degree or diploma. The reader I have had in mind is the interested layman such as a tutor or other person in contact with students or concerned to understand some aspects of them. In some slight way a doctor or nurse entering student health might find the text of value. Counsellors and career officers might also welcome the view of medicine as applied to student health that I have tried to provide.

My aim has been to promote understanding rather than to lay down rules or procedures. Others may disagree with some of the views expressed but the purpose has not been to teach readers to be doctors but simply to enlarge areas of understanding and comprehension. At the lowest level of all the book might assist in interpreting medical reports. Next it might furnish information which could allow the tutor to decide whether a medical condition is present or whether the doctor might be able to be of assistance. Finally, it should explain the source of some of the doctors' difficulties and irritating attitudes.

Some of my psychiatric views derived from dealing with students are perhaps a little unorthodox and original to the extent that I am unaware of publication elsewhere, but, in view of the enormous output of medical articles it is rapidly becoming impossible to be sure of what is known. I have therefore had to rely upon my own experience, observations and deductions to a slightly greater extent than may be wise. There are also a number of deliberate omissions the only excuse for which is that I find it impossible to write about anything I don't believe. However, I would not claim to be free of all delusions.

Some readers may be upset by frequent references to sex; but sex is an important part of the whole adolescent. Experience in student health and elsewhere has convinced me, long ago, that sex and sexuality (and not just genitality) are the largely uncharted areas in which our next preventive steps must be taken. I do not mean this in only the obvious sense of V.D. and population control, or even in the technical sense of eliminating the unnecessary sexual difficulties which are the scourge of so many marriages and the source of so much distress but in a still deeper sense which is to do with personality formation, with interpersonal relationships, with avoiding the emotional and psychosomatic illnesses or, in short, with the removal of barriers to human happiness, human achievement and human fulfilment.

Freud led the way here but his name and concepts are often hurled around in argument like missiles at hated enemies rather than being used gently as the means by which we can understand and relieve otherwise inexplicable distress. To trample on Freud is to trample on humanity and to ignore large areas of human misery. He may or may not have been entirely correct but his insights provided therapeutic instruments at least as powerful in their own field as are antibiotics in theirs. Nearly everyone, whether they agree with his theories or not, makes use of his notions—perhaps without even realizing it—and to do otherwise would be the purest blind folly.

I am not a psychoanalyst—nor even a psychiatrist—but feel that some explanation of how I view and use analytical terms may prevent any misunderstanding. I have used few terms that a layman does not know or could easily discover the meaning for himself, but reference to the final chapter may prove helpful even to convinced anti-Freudians if only to establish a vocabulary.

The aim of a Student Health Service is to make available the facilities of medicine to the student. Now that so many of the physical illness which used to affect him are under control the emphasis has moved to the mind and those past and present experiences which can disturb its efficient functioning. Thus student health has widened its frontiers and is more intimately concerned with both the student's academic and 'private' life than in the past. Not only is the cure of existing disease involved but also prevention and beyond both these the promotion of efficiency. Contemporary student health work seeks to achieve more than simply making the student healthy in order that he can avail himself of his opportunities unhindered by physical illness, it also intervenes positively and directly with the aim of enhancing his intellectual performance and this, in the case of an obsessional, for example, may paradoxically involve getting him to see that he should do less work. Anything which diminishes the student's mental capacities or distracts him is of concern. He is likely to turn to the Student Health Service for assistance especially if his troubles have led to the production of symptoms. Student health doctors increasingly view symptoms within the context of the total individual and his total environment. Even small changes in either can exert large effects in terms of mental efficiency in the aspiring adolescent. This is making the task harder not easier since negative diagnosis is involved at the level of organic medicine. This means that the possibility of a physical illness underlying symptoms has to be reasonably eliminated before a more psychological one is entertained. Negative diagnosis is more difficult than positive diagnosis and the true task only commences when this has been done.

I am indebted to my colleagues in the British Student Health Association who in their writings and in their discussions at the annual conference of the Association provide different views and perspectives of the student and his illnesses; these have proved illuminating. If anything seems to be too dogmatic in the material that follows then I have failed to reflect the doubts and uncertainties which abound in student health work in particular and in adolescent medicine in general.

Amongst my colleagues I am especially in the debt of Dr. Nicolas Malleson for his encouragement and criticism. There is a temptation in student health work not to face up to some of the most difficult problems especially where issues of morality can be introduced into the debate. It requires some courage to deal with matters as they are, rather than as we might like to see them in some ideal world. Dr. Malleson possesses the courage and I hope this book reflects some of his example.

I am also greatly indebted to Dr. Christopher Lucas for general guidance and for help with some of the psychoanalytical material. His restraining hand has prevented me from making some mistakes and I am grateful.

Most importantly of all I am grateful to the students themselves who teach me so much.

P.C.

I

The Student and His Role in Society

THE student's role is central to the continuation of civilization. He is involved in the process by which skill, knowledge, and modes of thought are transmitted from one generation to the next. He himself is very unlikely to describe or even perceive his function in this way. In fact he usually thinks in terms of his aims which may be stated in a variety of ways but which amount to a desire to please his parents, obtain a good job, postpone entry into the 'real' world, learn more about his subject and some even think of the course of study as being work like any other work for which, they feel, they should receive a 'wage'. At a deeper level still, and often not very consciously, the student has vaguer aims which may well be of even greater importance in furnishing motive power. They are usually well concealed and are often in contradiction to his more superficial attitudes. He may wish to earn respect, or self respect, or 'prove' himself, or compensate for real or imaginary defects in himself. Success over a sibling may be important in order to earn more parental love. A higher qualification may obtain security or enhance his chances with the opposite sex. In daydreams he may see himself running I.C.I. or 'saving' the country, devising some miraculous invention, or discovering the 'cure' for cancer, or being powerful, wealthy or universally loved for his good works.

It is usually difficult to persuade him to talk about these matters at a deeply personal level but it is just at this level that his fears and aspirations, his motivations and the inner 'problems' that he is trying to solve can be most easily seen and assessed. It is the raw material of his ambition and if it becomes disturbed his efforts may well cease. A twenty-five year old Ph.D student who came to notice because of severe conflict with her supervisor and because of threats of suicide, turned out to have been unconsciously but severely jealous of her sister and the predominant motive force of her life had been to beat her rival academically. She suddenly realized that she had won by a handsome lead and her sister was no longer a threat. She had always ignored men since they were irrelevant to her main motivation in life but as soon as this was relinquished she became preoccupied with thoughts about them, abandoned her course and eventually married. Although basically simple such a case can be difficult to disentangle because the patient is unconscious of the real cause. The chief presenting features of this case were of depression and lack of interest in work.

To succeed a student must have some ambition no matter how well concealed it may be under a veneer of indifference or hostility to his course and future career. Loss of motivation is the most dangerous hazard he faces and everyone concerned with students should keep this thought to the forefront of their minds. His ambition and the motivation derived from it are the only forces he can mobilize to find the determination necessary to keep going and the resolution required to overcome his fears. It may be thought that interest alone would suffice but it is unrealistic to expect that the subject content of even the most narrowly based course will be all equally interesting to the student; almost all of them are bored by—or frightened of—at least one topic and frequently several. This is not to say that many students, perhaps most, do not have some love for the main subjects of their course and although they may denounce them as irrelevant or criticize the manner in which they are taught considerable enthusiasm lurks underneath. However, students are critical.

The Ancient Greeks prided themselves on accepting nothing in the unexamined state and a similar dash of scepticism is to be welcomed in the student. If this is not present he can only accept what he is told and the body of knowledge which is handed on to him will not be subjected to the processes of scrutiny, revision and refinement. The very act of transmitting information exposes it to challenge and may also raise enthusiasm to explore further. It is on these two bases that all progress is made and the seeds are probably sown in the individual during the days of studenthood.

The student is also at a stage in life when he is beginning to feel some responsibility for society, he is turning into a citizen. His curiosity and interests typically range far and wide. He may be distracted from his formal studies for weeks at a time whilst he 'looks into' some topic or other which has caught his imagination or engaged his emotions. He is full of notions and ideas about how the affairs of society may be better conducted. He wants to contribute and he wants to be heard. Discussions with his friends may go on through the night; the injustice he perceives everywhere may seem so intolerable that he must take up arms and become active in seeking remedies. Because he is inexperienced in the ways of the world he is basically unsure but by a process of reaction formation, tends to allay his anxiety with a display of strident self-confidence that verges on arrogance and prejudice.

There is that quality about any form of higher education worthy of the name, that inspires these processes in which all the past is recaptured and new answers sought for old questions and ancient problems. The educational institution should be, and often is, a seat of heretical as well as orthodox views. Academic freedom and freedom of speech are both necessary if society is to gain the long term advantages that education can afford but freedom can be dangerous for the student. He is sometimes too immature to take the best personal advantage of it.

The typical student is immature. One aspect of immaturity is instability; if it were not so then change, and therefore progress, would be impossible. To be unstable in a free situation can result in disaster. It may be the perception of this possibility which makes the student welcome advice from an older person but before he can ask for it he must feel that the source is trustworthy, free of ulterior motive, objective, capable of understanding and sympathy. This tendency is fortunate since it affords the educational institution an opportunity to help both its students and itself. The young realize their need for help and guidance but, for the most part, insist on their right to determine for themselves what line of action they shall finally follow. This, of course, is all to the good.

In all this the student is not really different from his non-student contemporaries. What is different in his situation and the special difficulties he faces. To him it seems as if everyone expects a lot of him and that he receives very little consideration in return. Because he is in a competitive situation even his friends can begin to look like enemies, his tutors like harsh task-masters who neither know nor care about his problems, and his parents like tyrants who have no regard for the extreme efforts he has to make even to survive. At an age when he desperately needs success he has recurrently to run the risk of failure and he frequently has moods when he feels the rewards will never compensate him for the strain. Usually he is prepared to work and work hard but the incalculable elements of chance reduce the value of the insurance that this provides.

Stories in the press of unemployed graduates and announcements by University Appointments Officers to the effect that graduates will have to adjust themselves to taking menial jobs in future contribute their quota of gloom. Students, too, are people and like everyone else react to current affairs. Some remain unbothered but others respond with anger or depression to events which affect them such as power strikes and devaluation. Both these are examples of situations which resulted in sharp psychic disturbances in a few students and encouraged thoughts of eventual emigration in several more. Against this background the student has to solve the same sort of problems as others of his age but in so far as these may disturb his peace of mind and distract him they can temporarily destroy his capacity to work. Students are usually too inexperienced to be able to cope effectively with two or more sources of real anxiety simultaneously and the one which seems more important precludes the other. Thus severe parental troubles, difficulties with the opposite sex, fear that his girlfriend may be pregnant, loss of valued property, being charged by the police and so on can all bring effective work to a standstill thus increasing his anxieties even further.

Some observers feel that since the typical student age group can span such a troubled time in life it would be better to postpone entry into further or higher education until later. Such a policy would result in fewer disturbances in our institutions and for some students a year or two out of college is to their benefit but overall there would probably be a loss to the educational process since adolescence is such an intellectually fertile period.

The question is commonly asked why students—and for that matter, adolescents in general—have so many problems and give rise to so many difficulties today. The answer is complex and many factors need to be considered. Earlier physical maturity leads to conflict with the parental generation who feel that their adolescents are 'too young' to be undertaking experiences which they themselves underwent a year or two later in chronological age. There is less shame in admitting to the existence of trouble and less strenuous efforts than in the past to conceal it, which is surely to the good. Increasingly high academic standards are required for success and there are greater penalties for failure but at the same time there are more distractions requiring more will-power to resist. The proliferation of alternative 'cultures' and life styles, many based on simple but beguiling 'philosophies', offer easy refuge from personal effort. In an age dedicated to 'security' the lessening of basic physical adversity in life seems to have the effect of reducing 'resistance' to minor psychic illness or alternatively of permitting it to flourish; there is also a reduced or non-existent sense of obligation and gratitude for financial assistance provided as of right by the state and local authorities thereby reducing incentive to some extent. The very size of many institutions reduces the element of personal contact between the teacher and the taught and whilst it might suit some students, for the majority it must be an important loss since the sheer friendship and mutual regard which often existed in the past is perforce lessened. An increased nervousness and tension seems to exist as much in the staff as the students compared with a generation ago; and there is increased hostility in the general population to students which encourages some of them to live up to the false reputation purveyed by the mass media.

Since students are all of different personality types the variation between them is at least as great as in the rest of the population. Thus there are to be found optimistic and pessimistic students, honest and dishonest ones, lazy and energetic individuals, courageous and cowardly students, hedonistic and ascetic individuals, self-disciplined and undisciplined ones and so on. What they share in common is to a greater or lesser degree their age, their intelligence, their purpose of obtaining a qualification and their problems arising from the passage towards maturity. The herding of them together in large numbers tends to heighten certain similarities and tendencies to conformity between them but it also exaggerates differences. Thus particular courses or years sometimes establish distinguishing group characteristics and certain disciplines tend to attract similar personalities, or, possibly, admission tutors see a certain type of individual as being suitable for that particular course. Most engineering students are perceptibly different in dress, speech and attitude to most behavioural science students and even superficial scrutiny would serve to distinguish most medical students from most students of fine arts and so on.

Accurate generalization about students is difficult and much of what is written about them has little validity. Nevertheless, the foregoing brief description does provide some basis for comprehending both the individual and the general troubles which arise in higher education. The origin of student disorder and drop-out can be seen and some understanding of how the rational can behave so irrationally can be obtained from it. Nevertheless no general statement about students would be complete unless it drew attention to the fact that they are a real pleasure to work with and quite why this is so is hard to explain. Lecturing to them is stimulating since preparation involves organization of material and their interested but critical attitude makes the occasion a test. Marking their examination scripts—or the great majority of them —impresses because of the underlying hard effort it reveals, but most of all the relatively informal interview or consultation yields most interest and pleasure. Within the space of a few minutes rage, tears and laughter may follow each other, depression lifts and anxiety subsides, reality and unreality jostle with each other, personal questions and shameful admissions may be intermingled, demands to be allowed to be dependent are succeeded by assertions of independence couched in terms which sound offensive and are followed by a swift apology. The child and the adult alternate; a witty and even profound observation may be followed by a banality and a request for simple reassurance comes hard on the heels of a boastful and self-confident assertion. A day's medical work in consultation with students is exhausting but it is not the exhaustion of staleness or boredom; rather is it like the exhaustion experienced in visiting a classical city where there is so much that is absorbing and fascinating that in the end the senses must be rested before justice can be done to further experience.

Perhaps the basic explanation of why work with students is so attractive is that there is a desire—even amounting to an instinct— within adults to assist the young although this may be tempered with envy and a wish to impose discipline of a type appropriate to infancy. Among the societal roles the adolescent student possibly has the hardest task of all in that he has the greatest adjustment to make to an increasing complex body of knowledge and a highly organized society. His station and situation delay his progress to full maturity so no matter how adult he may appear he is still in the last days of childhood. Watching children grow up is always fascinating but coping with disturbed adolescents is, as someone has said, 'an experience which constantly reminds one that there are easier forms of livelihood' (Holmes).

THE MATURE STUDENT

The term mature student does not necessarily imply maturity in the sense of personality development but rather that he is over the age of say twenty-three years and usually has some practical experience of work. In fact some mature students are very immature which might partly account for their wishing to be students. In some cases the individual missed being a student at the usual age for one reason or another and then decided to graduate. In others the student is set on a career in life but feels that this would be furthered by the possession of a degree of similar qualification. Yet others have become discontented with their lot and decide to change direction using a degree to assist in the transmutation.

Although the mature student may well possess more stability than his adolescent colleague his very circumstances and the underlying reasons leading him to want a degree are attended with anxiety which may be aggravated by responsibilities to his dependants who may be making sacrifices on his behalf. Often more depends on his success, so for this and other reasons he is probably more likely to encounter emotional difficulties but is less likely—out of a misplaced sense of shame—to seek help but evidence on the point is lacking. Not uncommonly he finds it easier to make friends with the staff, although he can irritate them with his criticisms based on his previous experience, but he sometimes feels isolated amongst students. In one case that comes to mind this feeling was so severe that the twenty-eight year old student abandoned his course.

Mature students often feel that intellectual deterioration is sufficiently great after adolescence to prove a handicap and, of course, if the student really believes this his performance and confidence will be impaired. It is true that the I.Q., as at present measured, does fall with age but this is not quantitatively great up to the age of thirty years and even beyond. The decline in I.Q. probably reflects a fall in the capacity to solve novel problems but the ability to utilize previous experience increases. For these reasons mature students are most likely to succeed with minimal emotional distress if they have high motivation, previous experience relevant to the course, and a record which indicates that they have maintained some level of intellectual effort over the years. The statistics of the Open University, when these are fully available, will undoubtedly illustrate these points.

Whilst all mature students are likely to encounter some difficulty in adapting to a system basically devised for the late adolescent—although the staff consciously or unconsciously tend to make adequate allowances for this—the older mature student can react with marked resentment. Some even become the focal point of the discontent felt by all members of their course. One reason is that the mature student is frequently approached for advice by his fellow students who have a natural tendency to trust him. He may then take action on their behalf and make use of their complaints to express his own hostility towards the staff indirectly, but safely. In other cases the mature student may have had a definite role and authority before he came into higher education and the loss of it can lead to confused feelings about his own identity.

Undertaking a three year, or longer, course is a formidable business and the mature student deserves respect for making the effort. Quite often he is the object of a certain amount of admiration from younger students for this reason.

THE POSTGRADUATE STUDENT

The postgraduate student, who is typically aged between twenty-one to twenty-five years, usually encounters fewer problems than he did as an undergraduate. He is less likely to need help. His relationship with the staff is likely to be more close and personal than it was earlier and occasionally this leads to severe personality clashes which have to be resolved if the student's work is not to suffer.

Rather surprisingly at first sight, postgraduate students of both sexes can present with all the maturational problems appropriate to the adolescent. This is sometimes due to the student being immature in terms of sexual/emotional/personality development and he is simply a late developer whereas in others the student has been over attentive to his work—or has used it as a refuge—and so faces natural biological pressures for a close heterosexual relationship but is inadequate to meet the stresses involved. In one such case the twenty-three year old postgraduate student became infatuated with a postgraduate girl to whom he had barely spoken —and who, significantly, was lesbian—with catastrophic consequences for his work. His ill-judged, and ill-managed approaches were rejected and ultimately he abandoned his course feeling both a fool and a failure.

Work difficulties as such are fairly uncommon amongst postgraduate students but can arise. On some examinable courses a student who had no difficulty as an undergraduate can develop severe exam strain. The converse situation also arises. By and large the majority of difficulties arise in older postgraduate students who face some of the problems of the mature student.

The Overseas Student

Whether undergraduate or postgraduate, married or unmarried, mature or immature, English speaking or not, all overseas students have to endure considerable difficulty in accommodating themselves to the ways of a strange country and a strange institution without the support previously supplied by their families. A few adjust with great ease and in no time have established a circle of friends and a wealth of interests but for the majority the transition is quite a problem. Even students from Canada, Australia and the U.S.A. may well be afflicted and for those with imperfect spoken English the problems can be intense. Often these are aggravated by excessive and unrealistic ambitions. Attempts to give advice based on the real difficulties which the student will have to overcome can be interpreted as a personal affront. Some are poorly prepared academically for their chosen course of study.

Accommodation and money are often acute difficulties but most institutions pay attention to giving or obtaining help for such students. A more serious problem—especially for females—is loneliness since they are severed from their families but may come from cultures which have conditioned them against easy heterosexual friendships. In other cases the restraints are removed and this can have harmful consequences. Mixing with their own compatriots again can result in as many problems as it solves especially if there are internal conflicts in the country of origin. Overseas students from certain countries behave as if everything they say and do is likely to be reported back. In some instances they are reluctant to return home and this can result in difficulties.

Because of their difficulties and, in many cases, because of the special shame that will fall on themselves and their family should they fail, overseas students, particularly Asians, tend to over-work and be poor at seeking adequate diversions through leisure. They can be extremely hard to treat and a further difficulty is that, presumably due to cultural differences, a given psychological disturbance can present with quite different symptoms to those usually encountered in the indigenous population. For example, there are diagnostic difficulties and treatment is frequently hampered by the extreme tendency of students from some cultures to defend themselves against anxiety by denial. A further trouble is an excessive tendency in some to ascribe the causes of disappointment or failure to people other than themselves. Cases have arisen where racial prejudice, medical treatment or the lack of it, failure to offer a bribe, bad dreams or evil spirits have been blamed. Unreality of this type makes it hard to induce attitudes and practices more likely to yield success.

Overseas students require more support and care than others. The evidence is that they do receive it to some extent but it is probably still insufficient. However, it is never in the student's interest that support is extended to the point where he is enabled to exploit his difficulties. Overseas students have greater wastage rates than all other categories and as a group are least likely to complete their courses successfully.

WOMEN STUDENTS

Women students seek and obtain more support and help than their male counterparts. This may be a cultural phenomenon in that our society permits women to express their distress more easily than men. Alternatively it may be that they do in fact encounter more troubles. In the undergraduate age group, that is, eighteen to twenty-one years, the female is more advanced in terms of personality maturation than the male. During these years she becomes ready to commit herself both sexually and emotionally and both commitments can give rise to troubles which interfere with the capacity and will to work. These problems are dealt with later but guilt reactions about sexual activity, technical sexual problems, V.D. and fears of V.D., pregnancy and fears of pregnancy and disturbed emotional relationships are all commonplace. Depression and anxiety are more commonly reported by women students as are parental difficulties. Minor illnesses and worries upset women students more than men and the actual degree of emotional upset arising from a given circumstance is greater. Thus many women but no men students reported disturbed sleep and nightmares after a corpse had been discovered in a certain area of the University and several women took routes through the building which avoided the area.

Some women students have little real interest in their course and their intention in undertaking further or higher education is to be in proximity to men. The majority, however, are probably more hard-working than the male and seem capable of more sustained effort. Unwanted pregnancy apart they are less likely to get into serious trouble, with drugs for example, and are generally more attentive to the opinions of others. They are more likely to take prescribed treatment conscientiously and so tend to make better patients than men but at the same time are more impressionable and are more likely to become involved in religious activities of various types—spiritualism, witchcraft and black magic etc.

Some members of staff are hostile to female students, especially those who they see as manipulative. What is deemed to be sexual misbehaviour can be held against a woman student and some colleges—especially those run by women—can be positively primitive in the harshness with which they deal with these 'offences'. On the other hand some late adolescent female students, with their preference for older men, can be very seductive in the attentions they pay to male staff and occasionally this is calculated.

Because the attitudes which are adopted by others towards her are so important to her a woman student usually has to have fairly complete trust before she will reveal her full problems. A certain amount of astuteness is necessary to evaluate her symptoms and determine the true underlying causes of her distress. In a sense she makes it easy to fob her off but her problems then continue and re-present themselves in another guise. Sometimes she is simply seeking authority for a course of action she has decided to undertake anyway and this can lead to considerable misrepresentation of what has been said to her. This particularly applies to sexual matters and career decisions. For example, she may want to leave her course but wishes to do so in a way which leaves the responsibility with someone else in order that her parents are not directly cross with her. Although fairly transparent her underlying motives can be mainly unconscious.

As a group women students need more care if they are to achieve their best. Individually they suffer if they cannot establish a few close relationships both with their own sex and the opposite one. The vast majority have a positive need for intimacy if good mental health is to be maintained. In the student age group thoughts of marriage are usual (but are often denied) and this exerts its effect on them as does the menstrual cycle. Not only does this influence emotions, mood and behaviour throughout the cycle but in and around the time of menstruation, performance can be significantly impaired. The Student Health Service can help to offset this disadvantage during examinations and it is only fair that examiners should be prepared to make some allowance for it where necessary. Based on her emotional state, attitudes and previous menstrual history a doctor can usually make some sort of estimate of the amount of allowance that should be made.

Some women students are possibly involved in higher education in order to satisfy unconscious motives arising from difficulty in accepting her sexual role. She may, often at the instigation of her mother, be proving that she is or can be as good if not better than a boy. Occasionally she might, again unconsciously, be trying to make herself more acceptable to her father who in reality wanted a boy and indeed in some respects may have reared her as one. In one such case the girl's father was an engineer and she was on an engineering course. An example of her father's attitude arose when she had wanted a bicycle as a child. He had forced her to take a paper round until she had saved enough to purchase an expensive and complicated model which he made her dismantle and reassemble before first allowing her to ride it. She reported to the Health Service in a state of anxiety and total confusion about herself and her female role in her final year as she had found, or rather had been found, by a boyfriend with whom she had fallen in love. Conversely, most women students have to reconcile their passive feminine and home making reproductive needs with 'masculine' career aspirations and conflict between the two roles can result in distraction and distress.

THE HOME-BASED STUDENT

There is evidence (Wankowski) that students who live at home or near their homes have better than average chances of completing their courses successfully. This fact combined with the high cost to the taxpayer of providing accommodation for students living away from home makes it seem reasonable to require universities to recruit a higher proportion of their students locally. However, students who can and do live at home may well be different in some way to those who do not; for example, they may be less mature and more dependent, or their homes may be exceptionally happy. It is therefore fallacious to conclude that the majority of students would fare better if they were home based.

MARRIED STUDENTS

Apart from mature students marriage was rare amongst students a generation ago. It is now more common. Personal under-confidence and sex guilt are frequent underlying incentives to early marriage and neither is very conducive to marital harmony. Troubles are therefore frequent amongst married students as they are amongst the married young in general. Immaturity, divergent development, sexual inadequacy and, above all perhaps, children are prime sources of conflict. If both parties are students and there are no children, marriage may be equivalent to living together and is often advantageous in several ways. However, where one partner is not a student or graduate then the devotion of the other to work can result in frustration. In these situations the neglected party may seek extra-marital satisfaction. This then leads on to separation and divorce which are common endings to too early marriage. Often one party is very unwilling for the relationship to end and where this is the student—which it seems to be more often than not—work disturbance is inevitable.

A girl may utilize marriage (or pregnancy) as a means of escape from her course and married male students occasionally make their wife's reaction an excuse for withdrawal. The converse also happens and a man who perhaps lacks the tenacity of nerve to continue is assisted to do so by his wife. In other cases the wife's earnings make it possible for the husband to undertake his course in some comfort and for some mature and postgraduate students her support is vital.

In spite of nearly everything being against it some student marriages do flourish and are a success.

THE DISABLED STUDENT

Where a disabled person has the motivation and the ability a suitable course in higher education is likely to prove a sound investment both for the individual and society. The problems which often have to be solved are formidable unless the university buildings have been designed to cope with wheelchairs and accommodation suitable to the disability can be provided. Such students develop a good deal of self-reliance and display considerable ingenuity in helping themselves overcome their handicap. Constant confrontation with adversity may be helpful psychologically and this may account for the relative freedom from adverse emotional disorders found in many disabled people who have learned to master their difficulties. In fact the disabled students with most emotional distress are those with disabilities which are not normally visible such as sunken chests, hirsutism or a history of mental instability.

Some disabilities are a bar to certain occupations and this needs consideration whilst the child is still at school. Thus one epileptic student graduated before he was informed that he was unlikely to be accepted for the career he had always wanted—teaching. In another case a haemophiliac boy had been permitted by his school to prepare himself for admission to a geology course.

Although some institutions may be unduly cautious about accepting the disabled, an administrative problem which arises is the question of legal liability for self-injury or damage to others. The Open University should enable many disabled people who would not perhaps contemplate facing the difficulties of an ordinary College or University education to obtain a degree.

COLLEGE STUDENTS

The majority of college students—especially those on degree courses—are indistinguishable from university students. Their problems, attitudes and general abilities are identical or nearly identical with those of university students. They need the same type of support as other students but frequently do not receive it. Since many of them are recruited from the ranks of those who have failed to obtain admission to a university a general sense of inadequacy and inferiority is commonly found. Because emotional problems—as distinct from a want of ability—are a common cause of under-performance in examinations it is possible that the college population may contain a high proportion of students needing psychological help than a university. With a little skilled assistance such students can often be enabled to perform outstandingly well. Many, if not most, colleges have poorly organized health and support services but the situation is improving.

The problems which once beset student health such as drugs and 'the pill' have now moved back into the schools. These problems are likely to increase with the extension of education and the creation of sixth-form colleges.

The Late Adolescent Student

Most students are late adolescents. Although it has been argued on anthropological evidence that late adolescence is not a genuine stage in development it certainly is so in our culture. The interaction between the individual and a complex society implies that a longer period of adjustment is necessary than in a primitive one. Even in the latter it is to be doubted whether the personality reaches full adult proportions at an age which corresponds to mid-adolescence in ours. One striking feature which is manifest in students from all cultures is the slowness with which the personality reaches maturity. Over a period of time like three years the difference between the late, or even mid-adolescent who starts the course and the young adult who emerges can be startling.

One characteristic of the human, and one reason for his enormous success as a species, is his prolonged childhood compared with other animals. This delay in development makes it possible to train and educate him to adapt to any circumstances or environment. Our educational system, including higher education, exploits this capacity and it may well be that with the postgraduate student we are now reaching the maximum that can ever be attained. In whatever way education is described—as a transmission of knowledge, as the socialization of the individual or as a transaction between the generations—it is fundamentally based on the special capacity of the child to learn rapidly.

Adolescence is the second half of childhood and throughout the process the individual is establishing himself in the large world using as a conscious and unconscious guide the experiences he underwent in establishing himself during the first half as a member of the small world of his family. Adolescence is marked more by rebellion and self-assertion than by the compliance and self-effacement of earlier childhood, more by reason than emotion, more by scepticism than gullibility, more by interests outside the home than inside, more by a striving for independence than an acceptance of dependence, more by questioning the rules than quoting them, and more by creating a love and sex life of his own rather than continuing to adore the love (and sex) objects provided by nature in the form of parents. The adolescent is more aware of himself, more narcissistic, more solipcistic, more capable of abstract thought and more creative than the child from which he emerged. He is more able to deal with his emotional feelings in words rather than showing them in his behaviour. All these matters must be so or individuals would be mere copies of their parents and would never have any impetus of their own to leave the nest. Of even greater importance is the fact that adolescence offers an opportunity for the individual to overcome any particular disabilities imposed in childhood. A child who has lost all self-confidence due to excessive criticism in childhood can regain it in adolescence once he is detached from the family environment. Wonders in 'psychic engineering' can be worked at this age and all manner of maladaptations to the environment and stress can be permanently corrected thereby permitting the individual to experience more peace, happiness and attain greater self-fulfilment. Conversely, the adolescent can injure his personality development by learning wrong lessons and seeking self-defeating, and even ultimately self-destructive experiences which later damage his capacities. However, adolescents will seek and follow advice if only it is made available in a form they find acceptable. Students wish to see the reasoning underlying advice given to them and particularly want to know that it is based on their own case and personality, rather than on some generalization or personal experience of the adviser. Lectures in old-fashioned morality are unwelcome partly because they are generalizations and partly because the recipients have heard it all many times before. However, anything for which good reasons can be furnished is likely to be accepted. If we do want to establish a new morality it will have to be rational.

Late adolescence is more of a stage in personal development than a matter of chronology. Most commonly it spans the years seventeen or eighteen to twenty-one or twenty-two in (at least) university girls and eighteen or twenty to twenty-three or twenty-five in boys but in some individuals the stage never ends and maturity is never reached. Neurotics often give a strong impression of immaturity. The late adolescent is almost always aware of the fact that he is immature and this leads to a sense of insecurity even with his own contemporaries. In fact sensitivity to their reactions to him is an acute problem and some feel on much safer ground in their dealings with adults. Experiences which are accepted by the individual as defeat are commonplace and lead to bouts of self-isolation. A desire to be left alone overwhelms the majority at some time or another. Late adolescents still display the insensitivity which comes from an over-preoccupation with self, dark suspicions about the motives and attitudes of others and a deficiency of full empathy. Fears of being exposed to ridicule and scorn exert an inhibiting effect and the feeling that he has in fact shown himself up as a fool can be sufficient to make the student cease all contact with his fellows or indeed abandon his course. In one case a somewhat inadequate but otherwise perfectly normal first term male student was only restrained with the greatest difficulty, and treatment, from leaving at once, when he heard himself, whilst in a toilet cubicle, referred to by two fellow students who were gossiping whilst urinating as 'that bloody homosexual'.

Emotional development, which lags behind physical sexual development, reaches some sort of conclusion during late adolescence and the individual becomes capable of managing heterosexual relationships in an adult fashion. The romantic fantasies and ill-considered relationships of mid-adolescence give way to a capacity to establish and sustain a real association which is based on something more than self-satisfaction. No matter how unconsciously, deliberate choices are made based on assessments of personality rather than just 'looks'. The need to love and be loved becomes fully conscious in late adolescence and provides a drive towards socialization which, in most cases, overcomes the inhibitory anxieties mentioned above.

Sexual development also proceeds apace and after the experience of advanced petting which nearly all girls and many boys acquire during mid-adolescence an increasing willingness to undertake intercourse becomes apparent. This is not to say that mid or even early adolescents do not go as far as intercourse (although copulation, which may be regarded as essentially a masturbatory act utilizing the genitals of the opposite sex, is probably a better word to describe the act) this is not the norm. Typically the eighteen year old student girl is a rather doubtful virgin who may well supply moral, religious and parental reasons against her own desires. She may even deny that her desires exist but most commonly asserts that she has not so far met anyone she wants. Sexual activity, which is still mainly auto-erotic at this stage, probably reaches a life-time peak in late adolescence in both sexes but due to the ease with which young women can deceive themselves about the subject published statistics conceal the fact. However, sexual need is another powerful incentive towards socialization in late adolescence and it becomes more possible for the individual at least to actively contemplate making use of the sexual drive as compromises are established with the moralizing anti-sexual conventions imposed in childhood, as the oedipal desires which were reactivated in earlier adolescence recede and as masturbation becomes an increasingly unsatisfactory sexual outlet. These developments can and do give rise to a period of 'promiscuity', which can vary all the way from flirting to full intercourse, in which the individual is learning about the opposite sex in a trial and error fashion. If such experience leads eventually to a stable and happy choice of a partner then it is at least arguable that it is to both the general and individual good—provided unwanted conceptions do not occur. Students—both male and female—who marry before working through this stage often report that they feel it is a deficiency that they should remedy.

As energy is withdrawn from fantasies about the future and is invested in actual plans, vocational choices usually become fairly firm during late adolescence and the beginnings of a final life style emerge. This is usually consistent with styles displayed earlier. Relationships with parents can still be disorderly and this is discussed later. Many experiences are still new to the late adolescent and indeed students are prone to be distracted for considerable periods whilst they investigate all the pleasures which freedom from immediate control makes possible. Full contact with reality is still hard to sustain in late adolescence and some of their wilder notions and troubles spring from this source.

Swift changes in mood still occur and indeed the late adolescent student can seem like a different person from one day to the next. Since the character is not fully delineated highly 'uncharacteristic' acts may be undertaken either by way of acting out an inner conflict in a piece of bad behaviour (rather than experiencing it internally as a distress), under the influence of others, drugs or alcohol, out of boredom or out of sudden release of previously well hidden aggressive feelings. In one such case, for example, a student urinated on his bedroom floor after being rebuked like a child by his landlady for some minor misdemeanour. These periods of chaos punctuate a basically rather fearful and conservative attitude towards life.

Although late adolescence is a period of integration and adaption it is still a troublesome time. It can be an ecstatically happy period or an utterly miserable one but for most students it is a mixture of both. Basically the late adolescent needs plenty of encouragement and a minimum of condemnation. He is still doubtful about his potential and has well developed faculties for self-criticism.

* *

The Institution and the Student

INDIVIDUALLY the student perceives himself as being at the mercy of the college or university authorities. Not only can they exercise power over him and enforce obedience to rules in the same manner as a parent but they observe, assess, test and judge him. They keep records about him and for all he knows these may be resurrected and the information supplied to others later. In so far as the institution can grant or deny its qualification to him it holds the key to his future and aspirations and in some ways the organization, or its representatives with whom he comes into contact, may seem to be hasty in judgement, incapable of understanding, unfair and arbitrary. Perhaps worst of all he may come to feel that the institution has the means to discover his central inadequacies and find that in reality he is unintelligent, unable and even mentally ill or defective in some way. None of these feelings are particularly pleasant but they can be pushed into the background although elements of suspicion and a tendency to secretiveness remain.

THE SUPPORTING SERVICES

The task of identifying and helping the student in trouble can be difficult and there is no means of ensuring that the worst cases receive adequate assistance from the supporting services provided by the majority of institutions to a greater or lesser extent. Some cases come to notice when it is too late to be of any help and it is found that the student has simply left his course often with little or no explanation, or he has unexpectedly failed his finals, or attempted suicide. Tutors are frequently surprised by these outcomes and often remark that the particular student concerned was the very last person who he would have suspected of having trouble, that there had been no prior signs of it, that the student seemed alright when the tutor last saw him two days ago and so on. The tutor may even feel culpable but he should remember

that it takes a degree of maturity, which is usually lacking, for the
student to relate efficiently to him because of his various roles as
teacher, mentor, guide, friend and examiner : they can seem to
be mutually contradictory and invoke secrecy. It is rare for a
student to inform his tutor of the full burden of his woes and indeed he tends to report his difficulties, if he does so at all, in a
highly selective fashion aimed at not discrediting himself in the
tutor's eyes. The very decency of most tutors makes them somewhat
inefficient in their role since they are much more likely to wish to
offer friendship or advice to a student than to pry into his affairs.
However, in one investigation in which tutors were asked to submit reports to the Health Service on their students who had failed
the accuracy with which the majority perceived the real underlying difficulties was striking although they were couched as un-
certain opinions rather than hard diagnoses. This would tend to
limit the confidence with which remedial measures would be
applied. Students, on the other hand, tend to delude themselves
that their tutors know little about them, such is the success that
they think their attempts at concealment enjoy, and this is often
projected as a complaint that the tutor is uninterested. Tutors
frequently believe that if the student is not obviously unhappy, if
he attends the majority of lectures, if he seems moderately friendly
and his work appears to be alright then no matter what problems
he has they can be of little practical import. Since students
try to live up to their tutors' expectations of them this is not always
a reliable indication. Sometimes, also, tutors may conclude that a
student is of insufficient intellectual calibre to succeed and so again
they may be guilty of neglecting him. In some such instances the
real difficulty may not be the intellect but the personality which may
be ill-suited to the mode of education offered by the university.

Over the last few years the quality of tutors and tutoring in
both colleges and universities has probably risen sharply since the
older tendency to deny or dismiss student problems is now quite
rare. This is probably one good consequence of recent student
revolts which, at one level, can be simply viewed as a collective
demand by distressed individuals for the attention they need. Since
it is sound sense even at an economic level to protect society's
investment in the student the provision of adequate support for him
is an obvious duty that the institution owes both to the student and
to the taxpayer. The most important of the support services is the
Student Health Service.

The Student Health Service

Most institutions have some form of health service and these vary from a simple first aid room with a Nursing Sister supported by an occasional visit by the local General Practitioner, to complex organizations found at some universities, especially those in the U.S.A. In some cases the Health Service and the Psychiatric Service are two distinguishable organizations.

Most, but not all, U.K. Student Health Services will register students under National Health Service arrangements and thereby provide all the usual G.P. facilities found elsewhere. Although very high standards of medical practice are achieved there is perhaps a danger that the purely occupational aspects of the student's need might be slightly neglected especially at times of, say, an influenza outbreak. In most units staffing is well above usual N.H.S. standards so this minimizes the danger. A possible alternative is for the university to rely upon G.P.s with some training in the special aspects of adolescent medicine and student care to take clinics in the health centre, under the overall control of the university's own doctors who themselves concentrate mainly on students with occupational problems and on preventive psychiatry, health and sex education, co-operation with tutors, and hygiene and safety within the university. Most University Health Services supplement their staff with the part-time attendance of consultants of various types but most commonly psychiatrists. This is a sound arrangement since it allows the student to remain in his own territory during the psychiatric consultation.

Whereas originally student health services were most concerned with the physical examination of students, the promotion of physical health and the elimination of physical illness, especially tuberculosis, they are now increasingly concerned with the application of medical skills and insights to the relief of psychological illnesses, emotional problems and maturational disorders. Much of the impetus for development in this direction came from the discovery some years ago that the student suicide rate was considerably higher than that of non-students of the same age group. The interaction between the psyche and the soma and the consideration of the individual and his symptoms as one functioning, or rather malfunctioning, whole is increasingly the perspective from which University Health Services and other doctors operate. The links between health and education go back at least to ancient

Greece although the association in more recent times had not been as close as then. In higher education they are being restored and the extension of the school leaving age combined with the ever earlier maturation of children will probably mean that the School Health Service too will soon begin to take a new shape. The possibilities are vast.

The Student Health Service must be utterly confidential as well as medically efficient if it is to succeed in its role. The student must feel safe there and to a certain extent it must be a place of refuge and sanctuary for him. He must know that his own secrets remain his—no matter how pointless the secrecy is in fact—and that relating them to the Health Service staff in no way makes them their property. If at all possible telephone calls about him to tutors and other staff should be made in his presence and letters to them should be shown to him in draft. Even demands that records must be surrendered to him should be met if they cannot be avoided. Students frequently ask what happens to their documents! Suspicion can easily fall on the Student Health Service and this is fatal to its aim of being of total help. Where many students lose trust in the Service, or its ability to deal with certain problems confidentially and effectively, statistics produced by that Health Service can seriously underestimate the prevalence of certain 'sensitive' matters such as psychiatric illness, pregnancy, V.D. and drug taking. The students keep quiet about it and seek treatment elsewhere. Similarly all claims by those at the head of academic institutions to the effect that such and such a problem does 'not arise here' are to be viewed with some suspicion. He is likely to be telling more about himself than his students. To greater or lesser degree everything happens everywhere and always has.

Not unreasonably tutors and others complain that their efficiency is limited if they don't know the full facts. Their attacks on the system of medical confidence are really a measure of their desire to help but no matter how reasonable their arguments may seem they are best resisted. Various ways round the difficulty include seeing the tutor and student together with, of course, the student's free consent (i.e. the suggestion is made first to the student) or urging the student to inform the tutor of the findings of the Health Service. Some Departments endeavour to solve the problem themselves by stating that they wish to take all factors into account when assessing examination or other results and therefore advise their students to keep them informed of their illnesses and other problems. When some confidence in such a system has been established it tends to work well and helps to dissolve the—surely artificial—barriers between students and staff. (The latter have been justly described as students who are simply further along the path than the undergraduate.) At examination times students are often eager that their affairs be revealed by the University Health Service in order to influence the Board of Examiners in their favour although there are a minority who feel that no matter what difficulties they have had to face it is unfair that they should ask for any consideration.

Another circumstance in which students request that information be released about themselves is in connection with job applications. These can give rise to considerable difficulty. In one such case the student applied for a post with a certain Commonwealth government. On his application form and at his medical examination he supplied lurid details about his symptoms of exam strain. An enquiry was subsequently directed to the Health Service about this and an attempt was made in the reply to place the matter in proper perspective. However, he was turned down on medical grounds and subsequently blamed the Health Service.

Although the Student Health Service staff need to be 'neutral' between the administration, the academic body and the students in functional terms they are always 'on the side of' the individual student. He is their prime concern and their clear duty is to him. This does not mean, of course, that they invariably lend any authority or influence they may possess to further the declared aims of the student but that they consider, taking everything into account, what can best be done to treat and help the individual student and then set about achieving it.

Some Student Health Services are also willing to treat the staff. In so far as it saves them time and promotes contact, trust and understanding this is a sensible provision. Making due allowances for the greater age, responsibility and experience of the staff and the effect this has on modifying their symptoms, the underlying problems encountered are the same as those of the student. This is scarcely surprising since the consequences that emotional and other problems can have upon intellectual functioning are profound and disabling.

As far as staffing and the Student Health Service is concerned it would seem wise to assemble a team of both sexes representing the main age groups, different personalities and various skills. This gives the student the opportunity to pick and choose, and the choice he makes may well be a good indicator of the basic unconscious nature of his problems (and occasionally those of the staff too!) This is as it should be since the doctor or nurse who can do him most good is the one with whom he feels most able to express himself.

The Health Service and the tutor are truly complementary and between them they should be able to deal efficiently with nearly all the problems which arise. In some instances, such as coping with the police on a student's behalf or providing evidence to support a student's claim for a continuation of his grant after failing an exam, they work together. Where the student gives his permission for co-operation between the tutor and the doctor, really effective strategies can be devised to give the student in difficulty maximum support and help. However, other supporting services are of help with more specialized problems.

The Chaplains

Although adherence to formal Christianity may be declining, interest in religion is, if anything, increasing especially in students. Where this is excessive or has peculiar characteristics it can be the harbinger of mental illness. Some co-operation between the Health Service and the chaplains is therefore desirable but it can go awry where any member of the Health Service staff begins to think that it is his or her duty to promote Christian morality. If the student wishes to consult the chaplain about a spiritual or moral matter he will presumably do so but when he sees his medical adviser he reasonably expects that medicine and not morality will be the subject of discussion. The medical staff can and should do no more than take the patient's own beliefs, if any, into account. Thus a devout Roman Catholic with a sexual problem must initially, at least, be treated as such and nothing should be said which either undermines or promotes his beliefs, and if he eventually comes to modify them for himself it is his own affair. Except in so far as moral beliefs are related to symptom production they are not the concern of medicine which in any case has its own professional code of morality to which it must primarily adhere.

The chaplains often undertake a good deal of hard work on students' behalf simply as an act of Christian goodwill and in this role they can be extremely helpful, at least to a segment of the student population. Some chaplains seem to thrive on controversy and whether this is wholly desirable in a student environment is another matter although a number of good justifications can be provided. A move is being undertaken to increase the psychological and counselling skills of chaplains to students.

The Appointments Officer

One prescription for misery and failure is placement on a course or in a job which is not consistent with the individual's aspirations, aptitudes and abilities. The highly intelligent can probably survive and even attain a level of success but it is probably in everyone's interest that every individual undertakes work which he can enjoy and which will yield the reasonable rewards he desires. Vocational counselling is therefore of importance and most Appointment Services concentrate on this work but also place students and employers in contact on a basis where both are likely to be contented. The appointments officer can help with problems of motivation where the student is on a suitable course but has lost his sense of direction. Some services become involved in wider issues and may, for example, treat problems of gender i.e. sexual identity and so on.

Counselling Services

Many educational institutions have some sort of counselling advice available. In some cases it is based exclusively on the tutorial system and in others it is so informal as to amount to an extension of the 'counselling' which goes on between students themselves. In others it may be part of the Health Services or an independent service. It may deal with all and any problems or it may be restricted to solving only educational and learning difficulties or it may be aimed at some special common factor such as the problems of women or overseas students.

A danger is that under one or another guise a whole host of independent and even conflicting services can come into existence, function in an unco-ordinated fashion and thereby fail to obtain the best value for the money expended. This can make it impossible to manage the student in difficulty on an efficient and economical basis. It may involve the student in undue expenditure of his time and it can be detrimental to the type of individual who likes to consult as many sources of help as possible and ends up in total confusion. Some counsellor/therapists give the impression of being much more concerned with applying a particular technique of treatment to all patients, or, as they call them, clients, rather than with the actual individual. Provided these pitfalls are avoided counselling services should prove their value.

The Lodgings Officer

The function of the Lodgings Officer, which amount to the seeking, supervision and allocation of accommodation, make him of importance in the solution of the problem of where to live which confronts most students at some time. He, along with Wardens of Halls of Residence, can be of the utmost value in drawing attention to students in distress and in providing assistance to cope with the more social aspects of certain medical conditions. The accommodation resources of the institution can be used constructively in several ways which vary from making it possible for special diets to be provided by selecting suitable lodgings to assisting with the management of students with personality disorders.

STUDENT EXPECTATIONS

The student's expectations are of importance in determining how he will adjust to the transition from school and family to the environment of college and hall or digs. The changes involved are not particularly difficult in themselves but many students are ill equipped to make them and the stresses involved can precipitate a neurosis.

Towards Home

Simple homesickness is not uncommon and, as Dr. Malleson has pointed out, the home involved is often not a good one. The symptom is based upon the anxiety the student feels about what he expects may happen to his home when he is not there to keep the peace, to assist in its management or even to maintain his status in the family against a threatening sibling of whom he is jealous. Some students are unable to cope with the anxiety and return home in the early stages of the course. Others manage to stay but feel compelled to return home at every opportunity. Normally this behaviour is unusual in late adolescents living away from home but it is often apparent in the week or two before exams when the student regresses in the face of his anxieties and wishes to obtain the comfort, security and reassurance that the home provided when he was small. In some cases the rate of telephoning home is similarly a measure of the current level of insecurity being experienced by the student. Thus the parental home is seen by many as a secure base to which one can retreat when life at the institution seems threatening.

Towards Work

Survival in higher education demands intensive work although many students pretend otherwise with the aim of impressing others with their effortless brilliance, or of discouraging them from working, or of providing in advance an apparent explanation to themselves and others as an insurance against being thought to be dull should he fail his exams. Be this as it may studenthood must be one of the few careers where little or no prior training is provided.

Some students expect to survive if they pursue modes of work that they evolved at school in order to pass lower level examinations. This tendency is often reinforced by the large volume of work required by most courses. Attempts are made to master everything and know everything but learning by first principles and reliance on deductive and inductive reasoning is kept to a minimum, at least as far as exams are concerned. Such students come to the notice of the Health Service because of the mounting anxiety and panic they feel at the impossible task they have set themselves. They are sometimes close to physical collapse since they use every minute of every day and as much of the night as possible to cram in yet more facts in preparation for exams which might be months away. Sometimes the picture is based on neurotic attitudes towards work but for the majority it is due to poor working methods in the context of higher education. The institution should probably make some attempt to teach proper study methods at the outset but it should also review the content of its courses to ensure that they are not so overloaded that only obsessional personalities can cope successfully with the quantity of material to be learned.

Other students expect that the type of close supervision of their work that applied at school will continue at university and when they find it lacking are unable to sustain an adequate work effort from their own resources. The real difficulties which are involved in obtaining a degree seem to be rarely stressed to either school children or freshmen. For most students it takes time to size up the obstacles and until this is achieved they can scarcely tailor their efforts in any useful way. Both under-estimating and over-estimating the difficulties can be fatal.

A related difficulty is where the student incorrectly evaluates his own ability to a serious degree. He may feel that the pace of his course is so slow or that he is fully familiar with its content—a conclusion he perhaps reaches after attending the first few lectures —so that he can miss a good deal and easily catch up later. Missing four or at the most six weeks' work in a session for illness or any other reason is the maximum that can be made good.

Work difficulties also arise on courses for which there is no equivalent in the school syllabus. Examples are metallurgy, architecture, electrical engineering and the clinical portion of medical training. The student has little real idea about what to expect and the actuality may be quite different from what he imagined. The difference may be intolerable but the real cause of his difficulties may not be apparent to the student. That the course—and for that matter, life in general—is not in the least what he expected it to be is a commonplace comment by students on all courses. Some are pleasantly surprised but in most it is experienced as a disappointment.

Towards the Institution

Most students are apprehensive on first arrival at college or university; they tend to do exactly as they are bidden until they have made an estimate both of the institution and their fellow students. A few may stand out by non-conformity and generally making their presence felt but most wish to get off to a good unimpaired start. They listen attentively and are generally on their best behaviour.

In some colleges and in some schools of nursing this rather uneasy and false situation seems to continue but in most the student soon relaxes and becomes himself. He begins to discover how far it is safe to go both with individual members of the staff and the institution as a whole. The students then become a body of individuals but considerable attention is paid to the norms of the whole group. Not all students feel at ease where the situation which is then revealed is totally permissive. Just as some leave in the early days because they feel unable to conform to rules, norms and requirements—in the modern idiom it is 'not their scene'—so others are distressed where liberty has turned into licence and no check is placed on the inconsiderate who are permitted to disturb everyone. Complaints about noise through the night, for example, are commonplace from students living in unsupervised accommodation and if it rested with the opinion of the majority, rowdyism would be severely banned after a reasonable hour. Living in a disorderly and uncontrolled society has its attractions but it soon becomes tiresome.

The student, like everyone else when they think about it, prefers to live within a structured organization with some rules. The rules can protect him from those of his own impulses which he fears but if the rules are excessive they cramp his ability to develop his own personality. How he reacts to rules will depend upon his previous experiences, his attitudes towards authority, the opinions of his peers, how reasonable the rules appear to be to him, the punishment likely to follow infringement, the chances of being detected, and the advantages of breaking them. A few students meticulously observe all rules but the majority break some at least for some of the time. A minority react violently against them and perceive injustice in them all. Strongly hostile feelings towards the parents and poor previous experience of authority contribute to this outcome.

However, it should be made clear that most of the students support most of the rules most of the time; that issues about rules are rare and that most institutions are as orderly and well behaved as anywhere else.

STUDENT DISORDER

Most institutions—whether educational or not—are very slow to adapt and change so perfectly legitimate complaints arise from time to time that the rules are no longer in keeping with the actual circumstances. Even good intentions can be misunderstood. In one case the lecturer in charge of a course and the leading student finally came to blows over misunderstandings and suspicions which arose from changes made by the lecturer to ease the tension over examinations. In spite of the inertia of the system mechanisms exist to bring about adaptive change where necessary and in the main persistent effort and argument will ensure they come to pass. Good arguments speak for themselves and do not need the support of riots to effect change.

Somewhat surprisingly student disorder has not revolved round good arguments or even any arguments at all. Most of the troubles have arisen from what have been described as 'sacred causes' which are concerned with emotions rather than reasons. Action—often violent—of a type that no sensible authority could countenance is

undertaken or impossible demands are made. The counter-moves
by the authorities are then used to discredit and delegitimize
them. Then, what often started as a minority agitation on a topic
which upset only a few students is broadened into one which
potentially affects all students and widespread exciting disorders
follow. All the 'causes' are radical ones with a humanitarian flavour.
The circle of individuals who start the original controversy are
usually politically motivated militants and their sincerity is beyond
doubt. Clinical observation suggests that they are often maladjusted
and consciously or unconsciously seem to perceive themselves as
having been especially deprived, unfairly disadvantaged, or victi-
mized as children. Characteristically they find close interpersonal
relationships hard to sustain and political activity is a means of
relieving the inner distress they feel. They have not learned to
contain ambivalence within their relationships. They generally see
other people as being either oppressed or oppressors, goodies or
baddies. This permits the former to be loved and the latter hated.
Most real militants seem to possess high levels of aggression and
also seem to be inhibited over personal love. Since it is easier to
proclaim, in effect, that you love everyone (or at least the real or
imagined oppressed) rather than actually to love someone in particular their behaviour and attitudes which can display all the
passion, ardour, devotion and risks of heterosexual love, provide
a symmetrical solution to the problem of love and hate. Since the
other students are in a stage where they are questioning society,
establishing their own attitudes and are still potentially rebellious
they can become recruits to support the militants if the cause is
well chosen. Nevertheless, even at the height of disorders many,
perhaps most students are not seriously involved and may well be
hostile to the disturbance.

The case for authority—namely that it enforces obedience to
rules in order to hold the ring thereby ensuring fair play, that it
protects the weak against the strong, and that it affords central
purpose and direction—almost never seems to be made out. Perhaps it is thought to be too obvious to mention but the purpose of
authority seems to be widely misrepresented and misunderstood
even by those who wield it. Without authority no organized society
is possible but nevertheless authority may, and probably should be
challenged and must always be prepared to yield to reason and
justify its actions. However, to undermine it deliberately when it
is fulfilling a proper function in a reasonable and not excessive

fashion is highly mischievous. Even so, it is probably no bad thing to permit and even encourage students to challenge the rules and actions of authority, but in an orderly and sensible fashion. Also much is to be gained by students if they are allowed to participate in some of the authority's functions and responsibilities.

Some members of the staff tend to respond in an authoritarian manner to any challenge and this is bound to seem inconsiderate on some occasions. It is therefore likely to provoke an irrational response and resentment. It encourages identification with the frustrating and hated aspects of parents. Yet other members of the staff may support the demands made by students and many more have a degree of sympathy with them. Some have even been prepared to participate in student violence. This is surely inexcusable if only because it gives sanction to the use of force by a section of the population who, above all, should be being encouraged by the academic staff to rely on reason.

Student disorder, in the United States at least, is accompanied by a reduction in the number of students reporting to the Health Service with psychological problems. The same phenomenon has been observed in the population at large during the troubles in Northern Ireland, but secondary problems do arise. One such student from Ireland who had been knocked down but was otherwise uninjured in a bomb explosion was still suffering from insomnia, nightmares, lack of concentration and extreme sensitivity to noise a year after the event. Student disorders probably relieve boredom, permit the release of aggression, give a sense of purpose and a sense of belonging to a group which affords a temporary solution to an identity problem. A closer study of the situation may provide information of value not only to preventive psychiatry but also to the prevention of disorder.

Student Safety

Whilst educational institutions do not seem to be particularly dangerous as judged from the number and severity of the accidents and related misfortunes which are reported, many are more potentially dangerous than most factories. This follows from the huge variety of chemical, mechanical, electrical, bacteriological and radiological hazards that can be found in many such institutions. Most of the apparatus, processes and materials are in experimental form. Some are novel and no information exists about their possible adverse medical effects.

Students, especially new ones, may be naive about the risks to which they are exposed and in any case the most careful supervision in the laboratory and workshop will not always prevent mistakes being made and danger arising. The deliberate misuse of appliances and substances is quite rare.

The first thing that a student should learn about any dangerous process is how to protect himself and others from harm and the action to be taken in an emergency. Examiners could probably do more to help by setting questions or part-questions about safe procedures. However, safety as such does not have a great appeal to most students so the approach should be mainly through professional pride i.e. the issue is basically one for the academic staff rather than the Safety or Health Protection Officer.

Two special aspects of safety for students relate to their use as experimental subjects and to expeditions. Where exposure to drugs, deprivation of any kind, any form of endurance, dangerous stimuli or possible psychic trauma is involved the use of students experimentally should be subject to medical approval or even supervision. Most students are only too willing to help in research projects but may be medically unsuitable for one reason or another. The mortality and morbidity rate on student expeditions does seem to be somewhat high and some medical control is desirable.

FINANCIAL PROBLEMS

Attendance at college or university is usually the first time in his life that the student has to take responsibility for his own financial affairs. Since he is a learner mismanagement is common but parents and indulgent bank managers (who hope to obtain the student's account for life) usually protect him from the worst consequences. However, money matters can affect both his health and his capacity to work.

If he is short of money either due to mismanagement or because his parents refuse to pay their full contribution towards his grant— which is not uncommon—or because he prefers to spend an excessive proportion of his income on inessentials, then his diet may suffer. Dietary advice of one sort or another is required by a surprisingly large proportion of students, especially those who cater for themselves. Similarly if he is in a poor financial state he may attempt to find a part-time job which usually encroaches on his time for study and relaxation. A too large proportion of his vacation may be spent in earning money and this to the detriment of some activity which would be more personally profitable to him. Neurotic reactions precipitated by money problems do arise especially in girls and can be difficult to treat. Many girls have difficulty in controlling their expenditure on clothes and it is hard not to sympathize with them. The other situation which is likely to provoke a money crisis for them is an unwanted conception but it is not usually too difficult to find some form of help. Some institutions have official or semi-official arrangements to make loans for the purpose of obtaining an abortion and this is sensible. Some tutors are excellent at finding solutions to money problems and many are willing to give advice and supervision as part of their pastoral care of the student.

GENERAL ADJUSTMENT TO STUDENT LIFE

The problem for the student is to fit into the framework provided by the institution and this in such a way that the continued evolution of his personality is not prejudiced. Viewed in this light more liberal and tolerant attitudes on the part of the institution are to be welcomed since they permit more individual expression and encourage responsibility for self. In this way he can grow. When a student has done something stupid he is only too keenly aware of the fact and usually learns the appropriate lesson. He doesn't really need anyone to tell him so and to reproach him is largely unnecessary. In most cases the need is to try to prevent him from being too harsh on himself. Since the young are learners they are bound to make mistakes and to expect them to display the wisdom of Solomon is wholly unreasonable. The task is rather to encourage them to build up faith in themselves and to try by every means to ensure that they have some success. The agonies of disappointment that they can feel in themselves but also, out of pride, attempt to conceal are touching to witness. Their greatest need is for constructive help in the process of adjustment and no hindrance although some degree of adversity seems to be necessary if full stature is to be attained.

The late adolescent and the student in particular have so many adjustments to make it is scarcely surprising that their resources are occasionally overwhelmed and their reserves depleted. Even in this parlous state they need to learn to keep mobile rather than become transfixed or regress, and to move towards the real source of their anxieties rather than avoid them via a breakdown, dropping-out, drugs, surrender to the arms of 'mother' psychiatry as an in-patient or a thousand and one other but less dramatic evasions. For the first time they come to realize, perhaps only vaguely at first, that they are truly on their own and that they have to face realities which can be frightening. Others can help but the main effort has to come from within. It is no wonder that some students panic and perhaps turn fervently to a God whose assistance they hope to invoke (just as in childhood they turned towards their father for protection in the face of physical fear), or to hedonism in the hope they will find some respite, or desperately cast round looking for someone who might possess a magic wand and can be persuaded to transform reality on their behalf. Some find it all too much and work the transformation of reality within their own minds thereby lessening contact with the real world and perhaps becoming psychotic. These are all poor methods of coping but they are the best level of compromise which can be achieved under the circumstances of disintegrating defences. Often the internal (mental) forces were too inadequate, too badly deployed or perhaps previously weakened from either within or without to permit any better solution to be found. They may give way suddenly and treacherously at the first sign of an encounter or they may put up a stubborn fight making plenty of noise (i.e. symptoms) in the process.

However, the young possess the advantage of rapid resilience and rebound. They want to move ahead and make progress. Even psychosis, or something which looks very much like it, can be a very time-limited affair in them and an attack can pass in a few hours or days. It is possible that brief and usually undramatic lapses into psychosis or pseudo-psychosis are a part of normal adolescence but it is only the prolonged and persistent forms—for whatever reasons—which are so diagnosed.

In the neurotic student adjustment is again poor but the reason is that due to previous experience the distressing situation arouses special, excessive and inappropriate levels of anxiety when compared with the average man. Because the anxiety is excessive then excessive measures are taken to deal with it or excessive feelings are aroused in connection with it. Presumably everyone is neurotic (and therefore emotionally immature) about some situations but the true neurotic is perpetually burdened by his fearsome reactions. He can deal with these in different ways which will be discussed later. Neurotic reactions tell more about over-reactive attitudes towards anxiety producing situations (and therefore about past experience) than about the defences and forces available to cope with them. Neurosis can be very severe and very disabling; it is then easily confused with psychosis and in students the distinguishing between the two states can be very difficult. Sometimes (perhaps always to some extent) the apparent precipitator of the neurotic reaction is but a cover for an inner conflict which is most often of a sexual nature.

The adolescent has many adjustments and adaptations to make before he reaches a mode of living which enables him to cope with the trials and tribulations of life in a relatively stable manner free of major emotional or behavioural disturbances and moreover he must learn to accept the broad stream of life free of extensive evasions or inhibitions. For example, an individual who is unable to accept, without a good reason, a relatively free and satisfying sex life is inadequate; and one who perpetually avoids contact with any form of authority is disabled. Problems in relating to other people take many forms. One person may be unable to deal with other people (or just the opposite sex) in an 'equal' manner but always has to manipulate them, or seek domination over them, or make special appeals to them for consideration; another avoids them, or stands in fear of them, or seeks ways to punish them, or renders them powerless, or makes unnecessary submissions to them, or bribes them with offerings such as flattery and insincere agreement. Anyone who perpetually makes incorrect assessments about others (either good or bad), or who regards them as an audience before whom they must act, or has to 'save' them from their own way of life, or has to force their beliefs upon others, or finds everyone else a total unpredictable mystery, or has to impose intimacy upon them, or take something from them, or tell them lies, or is rigid and cannot adapt to others' needs, or has to try to force them into some role such as the opposite sex parent for example and so on—all these are deficient in interpersonal relations. Their perpetual problem is people and they have failed to learn how to act and react appropriately and flexibly. To some extent we all use these techniques sometimes with some people but where resort to one or other of them is invariable the individual is abnormal. Such a student has a personality defect and he is likely to have to endure some social isolation, or even rejection as a consequence.

The adolescent has to acquire a personality capable of dealing adequately with other people of both sexes and in addition the student has to master his subject discipline. He has to learn, as others have, how to control sudden impulses to revert to childish helplessness, to grab immediate gratifications or to lash out aggressively. He has to postpone present pleasures for future gains and learn how to live happily in the face of continuing anxiety. He has to learn how to accept defeat without despair, reverses without prolonged depression and how to pursue an aim continuously regardless of the immediate ups and downs of chance and circumstance. He has to learn that not everyone is going to love or like him and that it is a pointless waste of energy to try to make them do so. He must learn how to stand up for what he believes to be right and face, regardless of mockery, the threat of punishment or unpopularity. He has to learn how to like himself and overcome the self-revulsion imposed on him as part of the rearing process of childhood by the parents who did their best to socialize him to fit into society as they saw it. He has to accept that he is not bad for accepting pleasure, that he is not always selfish for wanting his own way and that showing off is not always reprehensible but is an important motive lying behind the drive for achievement. He has to learn to accept correction or advice without resentment or stupid negativism and learn that criticism is not always a sign of contempt or hatred. When he feels internally secure most of the time—which adolescents rarely do—introspection and the egotistical reference of everything to himself lessen and he can deal with others on the basis of undistorted perception which permits consideration, empathy, compassion and true love. He has to learn how to contain ambivalent feelings in a relationship without developing extreme reactions. Maturity also permits him to utilize controlled aggression in a sufficient degree to defend his own legitimate interests. The vague altruism of the adolescent should give way to the definite love of another individual and goodwill towards others. Tolerance and amusement should replace the sense of outrage and anger. People become real beings rather than ciphers standing for something or someone else. Whatever 'neurotic' attitudes his parents or others have taught him such as shame about sex, fears about money, avoidance of appropriate emotional or physical displays, excessive unreasonable apprehension about the opinions of others, disgust about excretion, unreasonable dread of doctors or illness, shame about psychological disturbance, dieting fads, over-protective attitudes towards the self, horror of unemployment, fear of authority, extreme self-reliance and so on should all slacken or even be overcome.

The student and to a lesser extent adolescents in general have to learn by exploration and self-testing their own strengths and weaknesses in all situations. They have to learn how to exploit their strength to the maximum in their given fields of endeavour and contain their weaknesses. They must accept their own lot, their own background and their own personality and not envy or imitate others to any unreasonable degree. Students whose whole attitudes, history, appearance and personality orientate them towards an intellectual life and pursuits, for example, will often complain bitterly that they wish they were like some extroverted, joking, girl-seducing, beer swilling acquaintance who they envy because such an individual seems to obtain so easily what the student wants —friends and admirers of both sexes. He hasn't perceived that his own personality will obtain all these for him and often on a more solid foundation than his friend. Incorrect perception of self in relation to others is commonplace in students. Real arrogance is very uncommon in students but its opposite, underestimation of self, is rife. Lack of self-confidence is one of the commonest complaints of all, but the student may compensate for it with apparent self-assertiveness.

Childish notions of good and bad have to be replaced by con-cepts of the appropriate and inappropriate depending on circum-stances and it has to be accepted that this is not hypocrisy. They have to learn that action, for reasons which are sensible within themselves, must replace action in accordance with principles or slogans if excess and injustice is to be avoided. The prejudices—of which the young are full—have to be modified in the light of actual experience.

Although many of these adjustments start to be made earlier in adolescence some reasonably efficient system for coping must be in existence if he is to survive as a student. He must be able to manage himself, his affairs, his work, his relationships and his emotional and sex life.

3

Personality Problems and Disorders

THE BACKGROUND has now been set for a more detailed examination of the plight of the student in a specific difficulty. Of course all students are in some or other difficulty all the time in the same way as everyone else but most of them they can resolve from their own resources or with the help of their friends. It is only when these are inadequate to meet the problem that the student may present himself for treatment or perhaps comes to notice in one way or another. Many problems of student life, and most of those in working life, arise from within the personality. The personality governs response to stress and interpersonal relationships.

In this field there is a tendency to confuse syndromes with symptoms and symptoms with causes. The same symptom or set of symptoms may act as the final common pathway for a host of different underlying pathologies in the same manner that fever and headache do for the physical illnesses. There is no common agreement in terminology and no universally accepted theory of personality development so discussion presents problems.

Another difficulty arises from the old controversy regarding the relative contributions of nature and nurture to the creation of the adult. In a physical context it is easy to see that a person may have the genetic potential to grow to a height of say six feet but that deprivation or disease during the years of growth may prevent this potential being exploited so the individual may only reach say five feet nine inches. The same sort of consideration applies to psychological development and raises questions about, for example, the fact that some people may have an inborn predisposition to neurosis and so exposure to only a little psychic adversity during rearing may be sufficient to turn them into neurotics. Others may have a constitutional resistance and so large disturbances may be required to induce a neurotic state. Slight differences in personality are found even amongst new born children but deductions made in working with adolescents seem to suggest, as has often been concluded by workers in other fields, that the young child is extremely sensitive to experience and small influences can exert large effects on the evolving personality. With age increasingly large experiences are required to exert a large or significant effect. Viewed one way it seems possible to perceive that everyone has some basic problem or problems which first arose in childhood and for which in one way or another he has been recurrently applying solutions ever since. This cannot be carried too far or all behaviour and character will seem to consist of symptoms but the central problem gives some sort of inner psychic coherence in marshalling effort, action and reaction. It is as if some basic lesson has been learned which governs subsequent attitudes to a greater or lesser extent. Thus, a particular individual may, for example, always seek to dominate others as if to eliminate the possibility of any threat from them, whilst another will take no unavoidable risks and becomes disturbed if his sense of security is threatened in any way. A third might react to others always as if he has the expectation he will be disliked and so on. These patterns can be very subtle and hard to perceive, but in those cases where they are markedly present their effect is maladaptive and a personality disorder is present. Some students act as if they had learned two such lessons and in these cases it seems that one or the other operates but never both at the same time. It can seem as if one is dealing with two different people.

A further possible aetiological factor to be considered is that of slight damage to the brain occurring at birth which might result in behavioural maladjustment rather than any other signs. The parents might react adversely to the consequent behaviour disturbances and thereby aggravate the situation.

PERSONALITY DISORDERS

Personality disorders are not necessarily an illness since many people who have the symptoms of a personality disturbance function effectively and with minimum distress. In fact the very way they function may relieve the basic distress, which is a sense of inadequacy, lying behind the condition. They all verge into the normal and in a sense they may be regarded as accentuated forms of normal components of attitude and behaviour. They can be viewed as a permanent disability arising in the personality during childhood in response to stress.

A variety of states is described under the heading of personality disorder or psychopathy. The latter term originally meant an anomaly of the personality but has now acquired overtones of viciousness and criminality and so is probably better not used in a more general way because of the misunderstanding it can cause. All of them occur in students as well as other people but their presentation in the student is often affected by his situation and, because he is not fully mature, their diagnosis can be difficult. Unlike most adult neuroses which start in late adolescence, the personality disorders are life-long. They constitute perpetual or repetitive modes of response to people or stress which are restricted, rigid, maladaptive and are frequently self-defeating.

Instability

These cases are psychopaths in the restricted sense mentioned above. They are usually male, frequently drifters and often take colour from their present environment being easily influenced. They are sometimes glib but insincere although they will make efforts— sometimes hard ones—under the influence of treatment to try to mend their ways and do better. They are egocentric and seem unable to act on what they can foresee will be the consequences of their behaviour. They are often optimistic about their future and it may be this which makes them heedless about their acts—they perhaps suppose that they will get away with it. A poorly developed sense of guilt, duty and loyalty combined with antisocial attitudes and impulsiveness are characteristic. A foolishly indulgent mother may make an important contribution to creating this type of personality disorders, but some people believe that the tendency towards it is inborn.

They are sometimes intellectually able and one such highly qualified student came on to his course from prison. He had charm but his speech was explosive and sounded violent. His whole history was one of very promising starts in the police force, in university administration, in industry and on two previous courses in higher education but always something had gone wrong. He felt someone else was always to blame but really the fault was based on feelings that he was inadequate and could not live up to his early promise. An 'accident' or an act, usually of a petty criminal nature, which he made little attempt to conceal and was therefore always caught, would follow and blight his chances. He had great faith in himself and his abilities until they had to be subjected to any form of test. He suffered from extraordinarily severe exam strain, which he endured with the aid of therapy, but failed his first year sessional exams. He was affectionate towards his wife who was a high salary earner and who uncomplainingly supported him through all his vicissitudes. The overall clinical impression he created was that he was good material and that if it had been possible to control his symptoms adequately until he had established a pattern of success, he would have gained self-confidence and solved his problem. Lesser forms are not uncommon and contribute some recruits to drug taking, alcohol abuse, student disorder, dropping-out, sexual deviation and so on.

This basic pattern, or something close to it, is also referred to as anti-social personality, sociopath or character disorder.

Irritability

Explosive or aggressive personalities may be sufficiently disturbed to be really aggressive psychopaths who may undertake violent acts on sudden impulse but in the more common form the picture is one of irritability, irascibility, domineering self-assertiveness, aggressiveness and anger outbursts in the face of frustration. This conceals dependent needs, insecurity and anxiety. A physically huge doctor of this type who frequently frightened everyone around him was himself terrified of the criticism and disapproval of his tiny wife on whose continued approbation he was totally dependent. Presumably he had managed to conceal his irritability as a student or he would have been unlikely to survive.

Irritation is a normal response to certain stimulations, especially noise, and frustration. It is highest in infancy and then progressively lessens. In students it may be well controlled particularly when the source is another student since to express it may lead to a loss of regard. Where inanimate objects or anonymous situations such as driving are concerned it can be particularly evident in those who otherwise inhibit it. In the case of timid personalities or in those who find some pleasure in the role of the long suffering (but sulky) minor martyr, irritation can be expressed, after a prolonged latent period, suddenly, violently and, apparently, very uncharacteristically. In lay language the individual suddenly 'went mad' about something or other. In a typical case of this type the source of the irritation was the family but the recipients of the resultant rage were passing cars which were assaulted. Men express irritation more frequently than women and this may be the reason why students, particularly girls, will describe their fathers as violent. Certain stimuli, such as that of a person eating, seem to be particularly prone to cause irritation. Anyone who is preoccupied with contemplating his internal anxieties can respond irritably to forcible intrusions on his consciousness. The need for concentration as at exam time, increases irritability and noise intolerance. The affected student feels that it is intolerable he should endure this addition to his other troubles and he may violently suppress the source of noise. Constant nagging in childhood is a possible cause of the irritable personality but the suggestion has been made that minor brain damage may be the cause.

Hysteria and the Hysterical Personality

The prevalence of hysteria which is a form of neurotic reaction to stress, is said to be declining with increasing sophistication and some people even deny that it exists to any extent today. As seen in students, in whom it is common, it is best viewed as another method of coping with anxiety arising both internally—and often pertaining to sex—and externally when the unconscious aim may be to fulfil a wish or obtain non-sexual support or affection. To a tutor and others it can look like malingering or 'neurotic giving way' to anxiety but this view is unjust since the relevant area of psychic functioning is detached, split off, dissociated from the rest of the psyche. Thus the advantage, or secondary gain as it is called, which the symptoms confer on the patient are not consciously sought. For example, one student became blind on the day he had to start his exams and many have a history of illnesses, to which somatic diagnoses have been attached, at exam times from child-hood onwards. Even today and amongst students masturbation anxiety can still give rise to crude hysterical symptoms such as blindness, debility and so on. Accidents involving personal injury are more common in the period before exams and occur to students who are found to have high levels of anxiety about the exams. Memory and sleep disturbances before exams have a hysterical flavour, and complaints such as headaches, dizziness, vomiting, muscle pains and lassitude are often hysterical. Many sexual disturbances in the young display the same character of secondary gain in that something which is apparently consciously desired but unconsciously dreaded is avoided via symptoms (e.g. pain) or dysfunction (e.g. genital anaesthesia). The clinical picture merges into psychosomatic medicine which is discussed later, but physical illness itself can provoke hysterical reactions. The distinction between the two is based on the fact that voluntary muscles or special senses are involved in hysteria and the autonomic nervous system in psychosomatic complaints. Nevertheless autonomic instability characterizes the hysteric.

Hysteria can occur in anyone, especially the young, but individuals who possess the so called hysterical personality disorder are, if the stress is sufficient, particularly prone to it. Such people are egocentric, dependent, suggestible, emotionally shallow (i.e. their feelings lack depth and durability), dramatic and 'stagy', prone to provoke passionate rows, fanciful, given to hyperbole especially when discussing their symptoms which they do in agonizing terms but with little evident distress, and they are preoccupied with sex in speech and fantasy but much less so in practice. Female students of this type are fairly commonly encountered. They tend to give a very misleading impression to men since they usually dress and speak provocatively but are often virgins or have severe pain on attempting intercourse. Their main sexual activity is talking and thinking about it and one way or another their fathers seem to figure prominently in their thoughts, dreams and memories.

Obsessional Personality

Obsessional personalities are found amongst both staff and students, since obsessionalism is not incompatible with high achievement, but most survive without passing into the full-blown obsessional neurotic state which, with its disturbances in thought and behaviour, is incompatible with academic effort. The obsessional personality is well within the range of normal and may be largely produced by the actual rearing practices of the parents. Such a person sets great store on tidiness, order, reliability, punctuality, the resolution of ambiguity, and perfectionism in general. Any failure to meet his own exacting standards leads to distress and anxiety so he is rigid and unadaptable. A change in circumstances can precipitate a crisis and push him towards developing in obsessional state. It is as if there is an anxious desire to avoid criticism for failure to meet the requirements he sets himself (or were set for him) and underlying it there may be a tendency to the opposite which if acknowledged as part of himself would bring harm and so has to be warded off with rituals or avoided through phobias. In part they are expressed in unwanted thoughts usually about sex, violence, death and God. However, in pure form the obsessional personality disorder is manifest only in attitudes and behaviour and not in obsessional symptoms. The obsessional personality is more likely than others to develop an obsessional neurosis but on the other hand most cases of obsessional neurosis arise in individuals who do not have an obsessional personality.

Students with obsessional traits are commonplace. Obsessive fears of disease (especially of the heart and genitals), dirt and physical decline occur frequently. Obsessional preoccupations may be used in an attempt to exclude anxious thoughts or memories. One postgraduate mathematician conceived, to her great shame, pre-maritally and after a spell of calculating the weeks from her wedding to parturition she embarked on endless mental arithmetic about the sides, angles and volumes of intensely complex figures. Similarly pointless rituals concerned with security, defaecation, sexual practices, washing and working arrangements cause distress and loss of time and are reported occasionally. Obsessional attitudes can also affect work directly as they did in one girl who had to write a 3,000 word essay but researched the subject so exhaustively and preoccupied herself so totally with it that she ended up with 15,000 words and a failure. Another, doing a course project in pharmacology, abandoned all else for weeks and even traced old and obscure references in the Latin American literature. Obsessional perfectionism can also underlie the inability that some students experience to start an essay or thesis or rather they make many starts but never a final one. Such students need protection from themselves. Another—very bright—student placed his finals in jeopardy by his obsessional thoughts that he had killed someone whilst driving to the university. Compulsive eating, common in girls, is another obsessional trait.

Sensitive Personality

Oversensitive or paranoid reactions are not uncommon in academic institutions where real or imagined grudges may be nursed and where suspiciousness about the feelings, intentions and motives of others may be harboured. They are probably the hostile component of competitive feelings which are unacceptable to the individual and are therefore projected on to one or several others. These feelings, perhaps, particularly occur in rather shy and timid people who are unable to accept their own aggressive impulses, presumably due to their upbringing. Within reason they are a fairly healthy way of dealing with interpersonal anxieties but in more florid form they can amount to fixed delusions. In one case an heterosexually competent overseas student who denied any homosexual fantasies, experiences or desires but who 'happened to see' homosexual pornography quite suddenly began to feel, after having been addressed loudly and critically in a public house over a money matter, that everyone believed he was homosexual and continuously talked about it between themselves only ceasing when he arrived. He began to search for official and legal remedies. Paranoid personalities tend to be hypersensitive, rigid and conceited but underneath they feel inadequate and ashamed.

The Weary Personality

The characteristically weary or neurasthenic student, who is not very common, copes with stress and anxiety by irritability, lassitude and generally by reducing his efforts not only in respect of work but also in his social life. His stress tolerance is low and he shows little response to encouragement. He wishes to do all that is necessary but is unable to get down to it. A proportion of female students of fine art, particularly, fall into this category and rarely survive the course.

Passivity

A passive personality is probably the product of a domineering parent. The individual is compliant and 'nice' to those around him since he dreads their anger being directed towards him. He may thus become timid and ingratiating. His hostile feelings are suppressed to such an extent that he may be unaware that he possesses any, but unconsciously he may be angry. Since a direct expression of annoyance is impossible he may express his aggression in a passive manner by simply not reaching the standard of which he is fully capable, set by the person towards whom most of his anger is directed, namely the parents. Passive/aggressive personalities of this type are thus a common source of underachievement and failure amongst students. Such students often ask that their parents be allowed to attend one consultation and generally behave as if they want the doctor (or tutor) to condemn the parents on their behalf. During such interviews the student may himself feel (unconsciously) that the situation is sufficiently supportive to allow him to express his hostile feelings for the first time. One such girl with aspiring middle class parents, and who had added to her passive 'offences' by announcing that she was in love with a boy whose appearance, occupation, background and mode of living were totally repellent to her parents, availed herself of the joint interview to use four letter words to her scandalized mother and concluded by aggressively enquiring about her pre-marital sexual practices. After some explanation which prompted understanding she became much happier, consented to continue the course which she had wanted to abandon, obtained a first, gave up her boyfriend and was able to express her hostile feelings, which soon abated, towards her mother. Her sexual difficulties also resolved themselves. In some cases the passive dependent needs are concealed under a veneer of disagreeable and sullen argumentativeness.

Over-Active Personality

Individuals who over-respond emotionally are called hyperthymic and those who are physically over-active are labelled hypomanic. The hypomanic is full of ebullience, energy, effort, enthusiasm and enterprise. Although they tend to over-value themselves they are often successful and failure doesn't discourage them. They tend to be amiable and get on well with people but may be ruthless and restless having difficulty in pursuing steady aims. Characteristically they rarely feel tired. Students of this type—who usually display the symptoms in somewhat lesser form than described above—are not uncommon but may have academic difficulties due to general over-involvement in a variety of activities. They may be officers of the Students Guild, have a complicated love-life and tend to be well liked. One such case, a parson's son, behaved as if any form of rest or relaxation (or 'personal' pleasure) was a sin. Another, a banker's son, who was consciously hostile and vulnerable to his father but who unconsciously had high desires to impress him was concerned with acquiring riches in the shortest possible time. His favourite daydream was of being wealthy and magnanimously assisting his impoverished father. In addition to his work he undertook investment schemes, bought articles in bulk and sold them individually, became involved in manufacturing goods and much else. He lived in his van in order to save money. He failed his first year sessionals but succeeded when he repeated the year.

Cyclothymia

The cyclothymic person alternates between hypomania and mild depression, highs being followed by lows. Mood swings of this type but of lesser form can be very swift in students but in the true cyclothymic they can last weeks, months or years being interspersed with normality. Usually they are outgoing, warm and friendly people, i.e. they are extroverted.

Depressive Personality

Depression as such is dealt with later, and here the word depressive is taken to mean an attitude towards the self rather than a reaction characterized by depression or a tendency to pessimism. Although depressives are prone to depression the tendency may be no more marked than in others. The depressive's attitudes are usually well concealed and many depressives are thought by others to be amusing, happy, individuals; indeed they may be the melancholic clown. The depressive is harshly self critical and feels that he is basically inadequate, unloveable and unadmirable. He feels inferior to others and is unsure about himself and his opinions. His estimate of himself is one of worthlessness but he may take pride in some aspects of himself. Depressive girls give unreasonably low estimates of their attractiveness and may have many criticisms of their bodies. Sometimes all their discontents with themselves are focused on one organ such as the breasts or the nose. They are insusceptible to reason. The depressive seems to regard as important not what he is but what he can achieve and so they are frequently ambitious but because even this seems to them to be unwarranted arrogance it is concealed. They find it difficult to form close relationships and frequently desire to be on their own. The sexual impulse is often singled out in a form of special self condemnation but they characteristically have indulgent opinions about the sexual behaviour of others, i.e. they are not prudes. Although the depressive may have all manner of achievements to his credit he holds them in slight regard and appears to think that any merit he possesses is shared universally by others and is therefore of little account. He tends to be sensitive and is likely to be prone to blushing which occurs when he feels he has revealed something of his inner, secret self. Flattery, gifts and compliments embarrass the depressive and such a girl who is told by a man that he loves her is likely to think that he is simply trying to seduce her or that his judgement is defective. Depressive women are often attracted by men who treat them badly since they then feel that they are understood and are not sailing under false colours.

The true depressive puts a brave front on things and everything he says and does is aimed at giving the contrary impression of how he feels about himself inside. He may never allow himself to show emotional distress in front of others and even the girls may make a point of never being seen in tears. There is an inner sadness and deep desire for affection which again is concealed. It often emerges as a deep love of animals who, in effect, are trusted to be more faithful and loyal at loving than any human being. The animal is felt to perceive an inner good-self to which the depressive's family and others are blind. Daydreams may be of the 'you will all be sorry when I've gone' type (perhaps through suicide) and are often directed against one parent or members of the opposite sex, which is a form of concealed aggression. Daydreams may also contain material of events involving suffering on behalf of a member of the opposite sex, which serves the purpose of showing the love which the depressive feels but about which he cannot speak. Typically the depressive obtains good results in examinations but believes that a mistake must have been made when they are posted. Depressives tend to dress neatly but rarely in attention-getting clothes.

Depressives are frequently the oldest child and are usually admirable people. By its very nature the state can be difficult to detect but it pervades most of the personality and the supporting evidence is found in the life history if a search is made for it. It is difficult not to believe that it is almost entirely the product of early circumstances of life, especially partial and perhaps unconscious rejection by one or both parents. Thus children who were of the wrong sex, for instance, often end up as depressives as do children who were displaced by a younger child. Jealousy, again concealed and usually denied, is therefore a common feature of the depressive. Presumably he was not permitted to express any hostility towards his younger sibling and indeed was told he was bad for doing so. Whatever the depressive is it seems he received the impression it was bad from his parents and thereafter endeavours not to lose more love and conceals his natural self. Hence, also, the emphasis on achievement in order to obtain love. Contrary to the child who gives up trying to meet the (usually conflicting) demands of its parents the depressive keeps on trying eternally and this is a characteristic of the personality.

For the same reason the depressive is sensitive to negative learning, since to fail to learn would be to forfeit love, and therefore the ordinary socializing processes to which every child is exposed, have disproportionately large effects. This may be one way by which the conscience, or super-ego, which is acquired from the parents can come to be more strict in the child than in the adult. Early adolescent depressives can be disgusted and ashamed about their own parents when they discover that they have a sex life; and pregnancy in the mother often has a disturbing effect on her depressive daughter's psychosexual development.

As viewed retrospectively through the late adolescent student it seems that the small child is sensitive, in a largely unconscious way, to the unconsciously transmitted 'messages' of the emotional environment. Since it emotes rather than reasons, the child feels that if it is unloved it must be because its personality is unloveable. In the case of the older child the loss of attention involved in the arrival of a younger one may well be so interpreted and this feeling was even reported by a student who was twenty years of age when her mother had another baby. Usually, however, the tendency to depressiveness passes if the child is five or so years old before the birth of the next baby. Mothers sometimes say that the older child should not have been emotionally affected by the birth of another child since she divided her time equally between them but even if this were true, which it cannot be, the older child has still lost half of the exclusive attention it previously enjoyed.

In late adolescence the depressive features of the personality usually seem to lessen and this under the impact of normal developments at this age such as falling in love. However, the actual establishment of a relationship can be extremely difficult for the depressive and any failure can aggravate the situation and any confidence is lost. This is frequently the story lying behind the attractive, older but unmarried woman. Presumably because of the tendency towards achievement depressives are very commonly found in higher education and there may be that about them which makes them particularly apt at learning. Perhaps because of their greater dependence on affection in infancy (and other ages) more girls are depressive than boys. The depressive will stand rebuke, in fact he only too readily assumes he deserves it, but his great need is for encouragement and more realistic self-evaluation.

In the psychiatric literature the word depressive refers to depression and is either used as an adjective e.g. 'depressive reaction' meaning depression or as a description of an individual meaning a proneness to depression. The depressive personality seems to have been overlooked in spite of its prevalence or it is described as a feature of neurotic depression. However, it is a fixed response of the personality and is therefore a personality disorder with the same relationship to depression as the hysterical personality has to hysteria.

A psychoanalytical notion which seems related to, or is perhaps identical with, this concept of depressiveness, is that of a deficiency of 'inner sustainment' from the super-ego. The basic trouble seems rather to be an inability of the ego to attract sufficient narcissistic supplies from the id and this then leaves the ego continually over-exposed to the conscience portion of the super-ego which in itself might be over-developed for the reasons given on page 62. The ego-ideal tends to flourish (because the individual is being good) and accounts for the areas of pride paradoxically found in the depressive. The Kleinian analyst's views of depression might also be akin to the depressive syndrome but they believe that all individuals go through a depressive phase early in life and if the outcome is not favourable the depressiveness remains.

Certain attitudes towards child rearing might also result in depressiveness, in addition to the factors mentioned earlier, and to this extent it might have a tendency to be culture bound i.e. our standard child rearing practices may favour the formation of a depressive personality. As judged from the necessarily limited samples that student health affords, depressiveness seems common in Western civilization and paranoia in Eastern ones.

Introversion

People with an introverted, schizothymic or schizoid personality erect barriers and place psychic distance between themselves and others since they fear being hurt, due to their early experiences of people important to them. They are shy, reserved, awkward, tense and may be eccentric. They may fear illness and brood over themselves. Although they are in contact with reality they daydream extensively of achievement that will prove their worth but often, in fact, seek isolated occupations. Close interpersonal relationships are stressful to them and even if married they are often withdrawn and distant from their spouse and children. One student of this type had acquired a veneer of briskness in dealing with others, which he did with some efficiency although never with girls, but his dearest ambition was to become the warden of a bird sanctuary. The only obstacle was repeated hospital investigation of his many vague medical complaints. Both introverts and depressives eternally 'sweep others with their antennae' looking for response to themselves, especially of acceptance and rejection.

Dependency

The dependent person is unwilling to take responsibility for himself and needs someone on whom he can depend for guidance, approval, criticism, love and general direction. It is as if he has no validity or purpose except in so far as it is granted to him by another. The dependent individual makes demands for support and may marry young in order to obtain it. A proportion of students, especially girls, are dependent, seeking someone on whom they can rely and who they can consult about every trivial matter involving decision. It is obviously a persistence of a child-like state and the student has no history of rebellion or dethronement of the parents. One student had her mother travel over a hundred miles to assist in the purchase of a pair of shoes. The dependent girl can move directly from parents to a husband but a dependent boy has a harder time in finding a partner who will mother him.

To a degree, presumably, all students must have a capacity for dependence or formal education would be impossible. One way of viewing late adolescence is that it is a culturally prolonged state of dependency in which the student is assumed to be 'socially illiterate'.

Inadequacy

Truly inadequate individuals are unlikely to find themselves in tertiary education because the inadequacy affects intellectual as well as emotional, social and physical functioning. However, there is a type of student who is adequate, perhaps brilliant, academically but in all other ways he appears to amount to very little that could be described in any very positive fashion. He is unassertive, unnoticed and generally overlooked. A postgraduate student of this type lived with his mother, had no interests apart from sporadically writing books and his medical complaints, had no desire for female companionship and disliked holidays. He lacked the ability to make any form of conversational gambit. This state had led to mild depression precipitated by disappointments in his research, which he did not pursue with much vigour.

Guilty Personality

Although everyone apart from some psychopaths feels guilt

there are individuals whose whole personality is structured around it. They behave as if they consider they have no entitlement whatever to pleasure, to comfort, to consideration or even to life itself. Self-reproach, self-punishment, self-sacrifice and self-effacement are important motives to them. They blame themselves or take the blame for events over which they could have exerted little or no influence and after the death of friends or relatives reproach themselves for insufficient affection or excessive hostility. They may even hold themselves directly responsible for the death. A student of this type said that reading or hearing of disaster anywhere—which, of course, is an inevitable daily occurrence—deprived him of all right to experience personal happiness. Several girls have been encountered who after some sexual pleasure have had their hair cut off. Certain styles of unflattering dress may have the same motive. Some students arrange their affairs in such a way that punishment, failure or rejection are near inevitable consequences. In one form prior punishment or the possibility of punishment permits indulgence in the pleasure. Clear examples of this are found in the sexual behaviour of some women for whom the possibility of conception occurring must not be removed. This is an important cause of unwanted pregnancy especially in the young female.

Other strands of guilty personality may underlie student altruism i.e. he is guilty about his advantages and salves his conscience by altruism. The selection of courses aimed at service to others such as nursing, sociology, theology, psychology and medicine may be motivated by it. This may explain why so many sociology students when they actually encounter the subject become disenchanted since it is aimed more at explaining and understanding rather than helping. Similarly certain psychology courses can begin to look more inhuman than humane to such students.

Depersonalization

The personality disorders are really developmental faults in ego structure but depersonalization is a transient disturbance of ego functioning. Complaints of feeling unreal, of seeming to be separated from others by glass, of seeming like a detached self-spectator and of changes in the body (the genitals being particularly often mentioned by students in this context) are sometimes made and may be combined with notions that the world is unreal.

These are depersonalization and derealization respectively. They are not delusions. They can occur in a number of mental disorders but also arise in students who are otherwise healthy under the influence of anxiety and fatigue. As observed in students they seem to be mainly a device for coping with anxiety and permit a reduction in the level of tension which would otherwise be disabling. For example, some students who are intensely nervous about the impression they create especially in more formal types of gathering such as a joint staff/student social say they feel as if they are floating overhead observing themselves, usually critically, but feel no sense of responsibility for what they say and do. Derealization may be due to the individual projecting into the environment his own unwanted and 'uncomfortable' inner feelings which then have the consequence of making the world seem unfamiliar and unreal. It can arise as a form of defence against feelings of sexual pleasure. Sado-masochism and self-injury such as burning oneself with a cigarette are associated with depersonalization in some cases.

Significance of Personality Disorders

All these personality disorders represent to a greater or lesser degree modes of coping with interpersonal relationships and the anxiety to which they give rise. They all merge between the normal on the one hand and the grossly ill and disturbed on the other. They all derive from an inner distress but the problem that the distress presents to the individual can be dealt with in other ways such as acting out, delinquency, sexual malfunction, or even getting oneself tattooed. Against the background of normal adolescence with its ups and downs, the stresses on the student may uncover, provoke or worsen a disorder in a predisposed person. These disorders are not necessarily in themselves matters of concern either to the physician, the tutor or the student but when they lead to social or academic maladaption or to individual distress they require treatment. The general aim lying behind management is to contain and control manifestations of the disorder whilst leading the student to a position of insight as to its origin and consequences. Because he is an adolescent, some disorders can even be eliminated but for the majority of the more extreme forms the disorder will persist and manifest itself in whatever form the contemporary circumstances dictate. Patience is required in treatment but undue pessimism is misplaced.

The symptoms of personality disorders can be and sometimes are only a part of larger psychiatric syndromes. Also they merge into each other and features of one can be found in another. The personality disorders are character adaptations to ward off distress so in their basic form the individual is not necessarily unhappy.

4

Emotional Problems and Disorders

IN one sense all the personality disorders are the part product of emotional disturbances during the years of rearing. In this section the purpose is to consider only the problems that can arise from what may be called the 'love life' of the student. Since emotional problems can seriously disturb his work capacity and they are of significance in student health.

Love is probably necessary to human survival both individually and collectively. The need to love and be loved—the mixture being in varying degree, depending on sex and individual idiosyncrasy— are basic emotional needs for which the human being is often prepared to endure much. The way in which love is expressed varies in different individuals and different societies. Words other than 'love' can be used to express the feelings involved and it is said that the word 'love' does not occur in all tongues.

Although sexual aims and wishes are associated in a way with all love, feelings of love extend beyond the boundaries of a male and a female of approximately the same age. They usually extend to people who are perceived as being similar to oneself when the word 'like' is used or to those with whom a significant common bond is felt. It extends from the adult to child and from the young to the old. 'Psychic-distance' is maintained between those who are neutral objects in reference to love but is decreased between those who mutually experience it. Love is thus a form of facilitated inter-personal communication in which warm feelings of affection suspend or partly suspend normal judgement and criticism.

LOVE/SEX EDUCATION

What an educational system might do is to address itself to the problems of maximizing the understanding of sexual and emotional life between the sexes in order to promote more satisfying relation-ships for the future. Contented men and women make excellent parents, steady workers and well-behaved members of society. Sexual and emotional discontent, whilst providing a spur for some, are destructive to the personality and the quality of life for most. Moreover many sociopathic disorders are probably rooted in sexual and emotional unhappiness. For example, one student who had a history of crimes against property in the form of breaking glass windows (their smooth, unperturbed uniformity annoyed him) and parking meters, reported with a number of vague medical and social symptoms. He was untidy, long-haired, badly dressed and alienated from his course, society and his family. His delin-quency reflected deep insecurities reaching back to childhood about love and sex. These received attention, his mood and attitudes promptly improved and he was able to establish a good relationship with a girl—whom he subsequently married—on the basis of his new insights not only of himself but of the female and the nature of love and sex. He became a model student and did very well.

Institutions of higher education are ideal for proper love/sex education because of the age group they serve and because their students will be the future moulders of opinion. However, the quickness with which the moralists among us condemn these activities as immoral, obscene, disgusting and pornographic ex-posed those who made serious attempts in this direction in the past vulnerable to criticism and sometimes threats of dismissal. Even universities feel, understandably, unable to resist such pressures and so little is done. But how and why it should be bad for anyone to understand sex and love is obscure although it must be admitted that some individuals with deep anxieties about such matters can be upset by straightforward education. The fault is with them or rather their upbringing, and not with education. In fact their only hope for anything approaching a normal life is re-education.

However, most sex education is hopeless and arouses contempt. Love is mentioned profusely, to reduce the antagonism of the moralist, but is in no real sense discussed. An adequate course for students must include anatomy, physiology, sexual arousal and response, psycho-sexual development, the evolution and purposes of love, establishing and maintaining relationships, the ideal man-woman relationship, the management of intercourse and the resolution of problems as well as the obvious topics like contraception, conception and, what is normally referred to in contemporary so-called sex education as 'making a baby'! Since such education, if properly executed, reduces guilt over sex it paradoxically reduces 'bad behaviour'. It is our conventional anti-sexual attitudes which promote what they purport to prevent in the same way as the clergyman's and doctor's tracts against the evils of masturbation not infrequently in the past drew the adolescent's fascinated attention to the activity for the first time. These tracts were as truly pornographic as anything that can be purchased from a 'dirty book' shop and their very production was a sexual act—although an abnormal one.

LOVE AND SEX

Since sex and love go hand in hand, inhibiting one inhibits the other or can lead to their becoming dissociated. In consequence, emotional disturbances usually have secondary sexual consequences and vice versa. In clinical practice one cannot be considered without the other. Unless more powerful factors intrude, the resolution of the conflict in the child of its sexual love of its opposite sex parent is probably more fateful for the future love and sex life of the individual than anything else.

To claim that students are all preoccupied with sex as some individuals who ought to know better do, is a travesty of the truth. Consultations where the basic concern is over emotional problems must exceed those where a sexual disorder is the prime concern in the ratio of five to one. Moreover, when due allowance is made for earlier physical and psychosexual maturation girls (who are always the object of principal interest to the moralist) are no different in their behaviour today than their mothers and indeed to assert otherwise is biological nonsense.

Refuge in Talk

The difference today is that the young talk more openly about these matters and in this respect they are probably more sensible than their elders. However, one contemporary difficulty which is presumably welcomed by the moralist but can be of concern to those who wish to see the adolescent mature in an optimal fashion, is that talk can offer a refuge from action and be a substitute for it. The boy who has friends of the opposite sex to whom he can talk about his 'problems' but no girlfriend is common as is the girl who has friends who are boys but no boyfriend. This feature might partly account for the rise in non-participatory sex such as films, shows and magazines in the same way that there has always been a market for non-participatory love films and books to satisfy the love-lorn. If the student is immature and experiences no need for a relationship then the situation is of no concern but if the conflict between his desires and his inhibitions is the trouble then treatment is needed. The student, no matter what face he puts on it, is usually under considerable stress by the time he brings his symptoms to notice.

The Inhibited

Since the adolescent is in a stage of development and is beginning to manage his own love-life any inhibitions may be something he will grow out of, and do not necessarily characterize him as an individual. Expressing love to a member of the opposite sex can seem a formidable business to the adolescent. For a girl in our culture it can appear forward, cheap and, what many most dread, be construed as manipulative by the boy. Depressive girls are so convinced of their unloveability that even discussing their romantic fantasies can produce embarrassment and reactions of concealment.

Many male students are still mid-adolescent and although they have their romantic fantasies too, and often more extensively than the female, they are still in the stage of believing that to show tender feelings to a girl is unmanly. They may, however, hunt them as sexual objects but their love fantasies are very passive —they want to be loved but are inhibited about loving. They often speak with contempt about girls and female emotions. In our culture rearing boys to be emotionally shy and emotionally inarticulate is the norm and the frustration it imposes might account for their greater preoccupation with romantic fantasies than girls.

Schizoid boys may have no great impulses to love but they are often desired as partners by underconfident girls.

Students who have reached the stage of awareness of the need for love and loving but who are inhibited can present with almost any complaints and symptoms. The cause of their distress may be inapparent to them. Bouts of depression can follow their—usually feeble—attempts to obtain a partner which have failed. Girls may cry themselves to sleep nightly and in students of both sexes, hunger for love can preoccupy the mind almost totally. Loss of a same sex friend to a love affair can precipitate such a state and also fits of jealousy, leading to guilt and anxiety, in girls.

Some characteristic patterns of behaviour in the inhibited include students who concentrate on the partners of their same sex friends in a flirtatious fashion but who are never able to make such advances on their own behalf. Inhibited girls of this type may endlessly assist their girlfriends in their relationships and thereby obtain vicarious satisfaction of their own needs. Another pattern is seen in the student who writes poetry with some member of the opposite sex in mind and so satisfies a need without facing the risk that lies behind the inhibition *viz* the fear of rejection. Those who have felt themselves rejected earlier in life, and rejection in a variable degree is one component of the oedipal situation, dread a repeat of the narcisistic injury.

In some cases the opposite sex is feared so much that the inhibited can only love at a distance. Thus one boy who had been desperately preoccupied with his need for a relationship finally announced, with complete satisfaction, that he was better since he had now obtained a girl. She turned out to be a penfriend in France. Inhibited and fearful male students may dress and behave in a way which invites girls to mother them or they may declare that they love a girl after a brief acquaintance. Such strategies are aimed at disarming the girl so that she will accept rather than reject him.

Purely physical defects can have the consequence of making the individual avoid emotional commitment if the deformity is not visible since there is a dread of having to reveal it eventually. Thus a girl with discrepant breasts or a boy who suspects his penis is abnormal may be overloaded by the secondary consequences and may even attempt suicide. Adolescents tend to over-emphasize the importance of their physical characteristics when considering their chances of obtaining a partner. In girls particularly any departure from the advertiser's stereotype is considered to be a great disadvantage. The catholic preferences of a physical nature found amongst males is a matter worth emphasizing in sex education in order to make girls more realistic and undo the commercially inspired underconfidence they feel. Underconfident individuals are more chosen than choosing and this is probably detrimental to their later relationship. It is very difficult, for example, to persuade a hirsute girl that some men, for their own reasons, find a hairy woman maximally desirable as a sex object and yet it is so.

Body Image

The way in which an individual, particularly an adolescent, sees himself physically can also influence his estimate of his chances of making good relationships. The body image may not correspond with reality and a perfectly normal student may use the distortion involved to express emotional dissatisfaction with himself in the form of unreasonable self-criticism of some aspect of his body. Conversely, the presence of a defect may disturb the functioning of the ego. Personality disorders are often expressed as disturbed body images in students; the adjustments that have to be made to the image in adolescence can result in feelings of depersonalization. Where the image is disturbed anxiety, depression and antisocial behaviour may all occur and the perception of reality may be unduly distorted. An attractive body image, which is first established by the parents, is obviously an advantage in interpersonal relations especially the opposite sex. It must be this which lies behind the observation that girls are as attractive as they feel and ones who depart considerably from conventional notions of attractiveness can be very effective in obtaining male attention if they possess a good self-image. Obese students sometimes say they are aware that their condition is deliberate and provides an excuse for failure in interpersonal relationships, an alternative satisfaction through eating and makes the body correspond to the poor image they have of themselves.

Disorders of Affection

The affectionless, and probably ruthless, personality type exists presumably due to severe emotional deprivation in childhood. Sometimes they are schizoid. All small children seem to develop the capacity to love but if the need is frustrated the capacity is eventually lost. Partial loss of the capacity probably explains the individual who establishes relationships but never injects any emotional effort into them and seems undistressed when they end. The same characteristic is shown by the mid-adolescent who can rapidly change his declared love-objects without much, or any suffering. After mid-adolescence the loss of a heterosexual love-object is always a serious business for all normal people.

As already mentioned the capacity to love may not be directed towards humans but animals. Similar perversions of love include the sexual love of one's own sex or children or of oneself exclusively. The capacity to love oneself in some degree is necessary in order to love another and during adolescence this occurs in the middle phase when the sexual love is withdrawn from the opposite sex parent and is invested in the self.

Some students invest a good deal of their love in some particular possession such as their books or records and if these are lost, stolen or damaged a prolonged period of depression (i.e. mourning) will follow. In some cases the love of their subject and of learning itself can largely eclipse the need for a love object of the opposite sex. In Freudian terms the academic subject has been invested or cathected with libido and this is a form of sublimation. To some degree these 'perversions' exist in everyone—it is only when they become predominant that the picture verges into abnormality.

Exaggeration of feelings of love is often found in students because they are still emotionally adolescent and they are 'in love with love'. Love may also be exaggerated as a means of reducing sexual guilt; a girl may convince herself that she is in love to relieve her feelings of guilt about her sexual behaviour. Provided a marriage is not based on it no harm is done if she can learn more about herself and love. An individual who has a twin or sibling of the opposite sex with whom he had a particularly good relationship can be prone to exaggerate feelings of love. It is as if they want to restore the relationship instantly and so are too eager and not sufficiently objective. The underconfident may exaggerate love in order to obtain any possible partner who seems to be available and this often leads on to young marriage.

Because the young are inexperienced and cherish notions of ideal love their affairs can result in distressing conflicts although the pair may be well matched. Because of the effect on work there is an element of 'marriage guidance' in all student health work.

Ending Relationships

Because the loss of a love-object is painful, because it wounds self esteem and because it can impair the will to work for months, the ending of a relationship in which one partner was deeply involved is a serious matter which is not infrequently associated with an attempt at suicide or suicide gesture. In addition to treating the resultant depression much can be done to prevent damage to the self-image if only the individual to whom the student turns does not dismiss his affair as 'puppy love' and his distress as something of litle consequence which will soon pass. In those who were not fully in love i.e. they liked more than loved their partner or those who are relatively affectionless, any distress may subside quickly but in most it can persist for weeks or even months especially if, as often happens amongst students, the lost partner is encountered from time to time. When the distress does persist unduly it should be regarded as abnormal and treatment sought. The prolonged depression may require attention but in many students in this state, the disorder is not so much depression as loss of confidence. The individual may be found to be preoccupied with thoughts and fantasies (of the *semper fidelis* type) of the past relationship, which might have ended two or three years previously, and which has been 'idealized'. The psychic purpose is to spare the student making serious attempts at establishing a new relationship for fear of rejection and failure.

The management of relationships, including ending them, is an important aspect of behaviour about which relatively little is really known. However, a few generalizations which can be of use in a sex education programme or in dealing with distressed students are :

(a) A good relationship is one where each derives advantage and satisfaction. If this is not the case the relationship is bad or non-existent.

(b) If a relationship doesn't really exist then the sooner it is ended the better : if it is not ended it will proceed to marriage, the production of children and then perhaps breakdown.

(c) A good relationship may be marked by complete sexual satisfaction but ultimately it is a question of personalities. Since sexually competent individuals can have intercourse with pretty well anyone else of the opposite sex with satisfaction, sexual satisfaction itself should not necessarily be taken as a sign that the relationship is a good one. In fact the sexually inhibited may perform better with someone whose opinion they do not value. Conversely, sexual maladaptation can ruin an otherwise good relationship.

(d) Blackmail of various types, including threats of failing exams or of suicide, or aggression against the ex-partner's new partner are unfair and even if they worked, which they do sometimes, they are only forcing the continuance of a relationship, which the other party has perceived as being unsatisfactory.

(e) The establishment and ending of relationships should be regarded as expressions of mutual appropriateness rather than estimations of personal worth.

(f) The young should try to learn positive and not negative lessons from their relationships and this will benefit their subsequent relationships.

(g) Patience, adequate socializing and realistic appraisal of self and the opposite sex are necessary if a really satisfactory and enduring relationship is to be finally established. The matter is of such importance that the efforts involved are well worth while.

(h) Although the average person is not fickle, our love/sex aims are capable of multiple displacements of object over a period of time. A common and comprehensible example which can be used is that of the dog lover who will never have another when his pet dies but soon afterwards obtains a dog of probably the same breed and gives it the same name.

Where the break-up is the product of a misunderstanding—and the young only have a limited experience enabling them to understand the opposite sex—then, of course, remedial action may be advised but before this is done an attempt must be made to try to establish how mutually satisfactory the relationship was to the individual as such. One observation of help here is the principle of homogamy i.e. the nearer the individuals are alike in all aspects— except the obvious sexual (physical and behavioural) dimorphisms— the more likely the relationship is to succeed.

Some students, due to their past, and particularly childhood experiences of love are 'neurotic' about the emotion and cannot tolerate any hint of anything that they can interpret as rejection. Over-jealous individuals fall into this category. They can be extremely difficult to manage if the affair ends and are often responsible for the ending themselves since they tend to perpetually 'test' the strength of emotion their partner feels for them. They are always a potential danger to themselves and their behaviour can be so extreme that their ex-partner is exposed to all manner of upsets or even harm. Such a boy may physically attack a girl or such a girl may take spiteful revenge.

Since all reasonable people will accept that an emotional disruption is likely to adversely affect a student's capacity for intellectual effort the fact is sometimes used, unconsciously, by students to account, in advance, for poor examination performance. Thus, accounts of ending of affairs increase before exams. In some cases the student perhaps felt unable to cope with work and a relationship simultaneously or work simply imposed too much strain on the relationship but in many the individual concerned seems to have precipitated the crisis and in such a way that the partner appears to be the one actually responsible. Deeper psychic motives are sometimes at work and a guilty individual may, consciously or unconsciously, believe that if he ceases 'the sin' of the relationship he will thereby invoke divine help and maximize his chances of passing his exams.

This aspect apart, students who have reached a stage of maturity sufficient to establish and maintain a stable relationship seem, in general, to become less emotionally disturbed about their work and to work more effectively than those seeking but unable to establish such a relationship. Since maturity is occurring earlier and education continuing longer probably a greater proportion of students need such a relationship than in the past and the tendency to admit more girls into higher education is one aspect of this. It is not difficult to see that the sense of comfort and security that students give to each other in such a relationship is helpful. Assistance with the symptoms and disturbances which do arise from the establishment and management of relationships is an increasingly important aspect of student health and work but many of the trials and tribulations could be avoided with better love/sex education.

PARENTAL PROBLEMS

Relationships with parents can adversely affect the student and precipitate work problems. In this, as in other areas, the Student Health Service must be prepared to deal not only with the symptoms but the underlying pathology in order that the student can eventually be returned to effective functioning.

In general it may be said tht physical, psychosexual and personality maturation involve the child in a process of increasing independence of the parents. A degree of conflict is usually involved but eventually the child gradually 'separates' from the parents in a psychological if not a physical sense. Where the process goes well mutual esteem and affection remain. Eventually, the parents, in old age are likely to become dependent on the child and the roles are reversed. Trouble arises where the separation process occurs too early, too late, with too much difficulty or doesn't occur at all due either to the parents retaining the child for their own purposes or the child clinging to them for his. Relationships between parents and adolescents are marked, as a rule, with ambivalence on both sides and are often conducted at several levels. Thus the student who, for instance, displays a lot of hostility to his mother may be overdependent on her unconsciously. The pattern is further complicated by the instability of the adolescent but in most families the basic desire on both sides is to be well thought of by the other. Adolescents are not usually aware of the sense of personal responsibility, guilt or even shame the parents can feel on their behalf. They are more conscious of the hostility, criticism and anger.

Since studenthood is a form of prolonged adolescence and since, in most cases, the student is perforce still dependent on his parents in many ways trouble is predictable. This may be of a simple variety, such as refusal to pay their contribution, which is occasionally based on hostility to the child or a desire to punish him for not showing more attention to parental attitudes about some matter or other i.e. it is used as a way to delay the separation process. Of course, it is not unreasonable for the parents to feel that payments by them entitle them to some consideration but using them as a means to seek ulterior ends is another matter. Some students, particularly those from affluent professional families, may reverse the process and at the slightest hint that their demands will not be met threaten to leave their course of studies. Others feel so unworthy of any further 'sacrifice' on their parents' part that they endure all manner of hardship and deprivation rather than ask for help. The underlying feeling is one of insecurity in their love.

A too early 'separation' from the parents and departure from adherence to their standards may be a consequence of a personality disorder in one or both parents or of over-permissiveness on their part, which the child may well interpret as a failure really to care for him. This can result in an over-readiness to adopt ways of life governed by impulse and immediate gratification. Whatever the exterior seems to be these individuals are almost always depressive or depressed.

The student who is over dependent on his family has already been mentioned. Sometimes this is caused by jealousy of a younger sibling. From these and similar cases it seems that the emotional problems presented by the birth of a younger child can result in jealousy but this may later turn into depressiveness or resentment against the parents, particularly the mother. In this way apparently contradictory attitudes involving dependency and hostility can arise. The poorly separated and dependent student often, paradoxically, doesn't want the parents to know of any difficulty in which he may be involved. This is in order to avoid the further loss of regard involved in 'being a nuisance'. The over-dependent student shows undue desires to earn parental approval and undue fear of possible criticism. He is therefore immature, insecure in his own identity and possibly still involved in the oedipal situation. He is not ready to establish an effective relationship with the opposite sex and is inefficient in maintaining a relationship.

Parents who wish to keep the child dependent, perhaps as a love object, or as a supplier of love and admiration, or for some other purpose may resent the student entering higher education. Some parents are even jealous and make trouble of various kinds. One mother assiduously reported all her daughter's misdoings and hostile comments about her course and the staff to her tutor with the openly expressed hope that the girl would be put off her course. Another, on the morning her daughter's finals commenced, savagely attacked and beat her with a cane. Other parents blame the institution for all evidences of maturation or signs of independence or every mishap that occurs to their child and fill files with their complaints—usually on grounds of morality. Some use complaints about their own emotional or other problems in a manner which when investigated is consistent with the hypothesis that they are endeavouring to make the student feel guilty and treacherous for having left home and so return. Girls, particularly, are subject to this form of undermining and the cause, in some cases, is the desire of the parents to depend on the child at an earlier stage than usual. At the other extreme girls are also more likely to encounter rejection for having left home, especially from the father, and on one pretext or another she is not allowed back.

Another sign that the parents wish to maintain the student in a state of dependency is the refusal to treat him as if he has no right to personal privacy. Thus demands may be made for access to medical records (but are always refused) or they move in on the pretext of some crisis and totally take over the student's affairs.

Parental expectations are another source of difficulty especially since conscious and unconscious ones both exert an effect and are sometimes in conflict. Further, most students have two parents who may have conflicting expectations between themselves. The commonest trouble arises in aspiring middle class families, such as those of doctors and teachers, where real value is set on intellectual attainment. Although the parents may be unconscious of it, the child realizes that achievement is expected and whereas all is well if he is emotionally and intellectually able to satisfy the demands, he may respond with increasing anxiety, depressiveness or even despair if he is not. Alternatively, especially where he thinks the parents are unreasonable he may retaliate with failure if he has a passive/aggressive personality disorder. Parental expectations can have very subtle effects which are hard to detect and verge on the unbelievable. Thus, the unwantedly pregnant or drug-addicted student may be fulfilling an unconsciously expressed wish by the parents and some cases of personality disorder seem to have the same aetiology. The hypochondriacal student, for example, may be meeting unconscious maternal demands that he be mothered, but at a conscious level she is encouraging him to be healthy. Problems such as bedwetting may spring from the same source.

Most direct parental interference arises from the relationships which the student establishes. Where the parents are reasonable people but their advice has been ignored events often prove them to have been right. Other parents fear that an emotional affair may distract the student from work and so oppose all and any relationships.

The death of a parent or some loved figure such as a grandparent can cause a profound disturbance as can divorce or separation. One very unhappy and insecure student dreaded her twenty-first birthday since her parents had agreed for years that they would leave each other on that day.

SEXUAL PROBLEMS

The prevalence of sexual disorders within the population is totally unknown but probably everyone at some time or another encounters difficulties in our culture. This is because our methods of child rearing attach shame, anxiety, fear and guilt to the sexual organs and the sexual impulse. This comes about partly from direct learning e.g. being reproached for touching the genitals and partly from the oedipal complex. Some people believe that some sexual disorders, particularly homosexuality, may be the outcome of inborn deficiencies or defects of a hormonal nature but in view of the frequency with which it arises this is a most unlikely explanation of the majority of cases. If the theory is correct then homosexuality is far and away the commonest of all congenital abnormalities.

As seen in students the sexual disorders can be broadly classified into five categories :

1. Those in which the disability is primarily concerned with the individual's own sexuality as such. For example, excessive guilt or fear may inhibit an individual's ability to accept fully his sexual needs or diminish his response and pleasure. The sexual aim and object may be normal but intercourse may be impossible or unsatisfactory due to pain (or rather pleasure experienced as pain), impotence or frigidity. The problem is one of dysfunction.

2. Disorders of sexual expression towards others. These two may co-exist since the first commonly results in the second, especially in the male. The consequence is inefficiency or incapacity in a heterosexual context and may involve directing the sexual aim towards objects other than the opposite sex, towards practices which do not involve intercourse or towards intercourse which is governed in some way by special requirements which must be met if the act is to be successful. The problem is one of deviation.

3. The disorder is secondary to some other problem whether it be physical, emotional, a personality disorder, or a psychiatric illness. Thus a man may be disabled by diabetes for example, by guilt in an extra-marital encounter, by alienation of his partner due to his jealousy or because he is suffering from depression.

4. The disorder is apparent and not real being based on ignorance, inexperience or incomplete psychosexual maturation. A complaint by a male, for example, that his partner is frigid

may well turn out to be due to his technical incompetence or her being insufficiently mature to permit herself to psychically participate in the act.

5. The student is a non-patient preferring to talk about his problems rather than make any serious attempt to resolve the difficulty. This is not uncommon, for example, in those with a hysterical personality who really want attention rather than a cure.

Assessment depends upon the nature of the disorder and how it is manifested, the psychosexual history of the patient and the presence or absence of related matters of importance. The sexual disorders have a double significance in students since their presence can cause personal distress and so interfere with work or leisure and secondly they are capable of remedy which may be impossible later in life. Since students are interested in sex and psychology and because they are intelligent and capable of insight sexual disorders are not too difficult to treat in them as a rule and student health, like the rest of the medical profession, is taking more interest in this area. The scope is vast and requires a book on its own so only a few of the more important general aspects are mentioned here.

Normal individuals are capable of fully accepting their own genitals and those of the opposite sex without disgust; moreover they can accept the pleasure the genitals afford and are capable of responding to those internal and external stimuli which result in arousal under conditions which are socially appropriate. They are free of undue fear of the opposite sex both socially and sexually and tend to place great value on them in general but in a realistic rather than mythological fashion. They are capable of discrimination between members of the opposite sex and know the type of individual who attracts them and they are capable of communication with these. Within such a context they can reveal their own sexual needs and are not repulsed by those of the partner even if in some aspects they do not conform to what is widely accepted as 'normal'. They wish to give pleasure and are eager to receive it being neither ashamed nor inhibited in revealing their response. Whilst they retain deep interest in other members of the opposite sex they tend towards sexual loyalty based not on the negative restraints of morality but out of consideration for the feelings of the partner and the pleasure that they can uniquely receive within their relationship.

Where disgust or shame regarding their own genitals is present —and this can only result from early training—this shows up in the subsequent psychosexual history and is manifest in a distorted body image of the organs. Some such individuals act as if they had no genitals and may complain of anaesthesia in the parts. Because of anatomical and physiological factors girls can maintain the denial involved more easily than boys and they may give a personal history totally devoid of any interest in sex or sexual incident whatever. They tend to be inhibited in interpersonal relations and, paradoxically, have above average chances of becoming unwantedly pregnant.

Where guilt about sexual pleasure is the predominant factor the history is usually characterized by excessive sexual fantasy, much secrecy, considerable resistance to masturbation or peculiar methods of masturbation. Self-punishment in various forms may be present. Such students present either because of some disturbance within themselves or because of heterosexual inefficiency.

In general both these conditions are avoidable if parents and children would accept sex and sexual pleasure as being normal, subject, of course, to restraint by social considerations. Thus it is senseless to represent masturbation, in either adult or infant forms, as being bad or sinful. However, the child may be taught to regard such activities as being basically private matters. Whilst it is unwise for parents to interfere in any positive way with the child's evolving sexuality (e.g. exposing it forcefully to sexual information or activity) the amount of negative restraint needs to be lessened if we are to become fairly free of sexual disorders. A greater awareness of the positive values of masturbation would be helpful in modifying attitudes. Guilt about masturbation is widespread and too many students, even today, regard it as a unique fault in them. Fears of the consequences of masturbation, or often 'excessive' masturbation, still flourish but usually in a more sophisticated form than in the past. Masturbation anxiety underlies many complaints not only of a direct sexual nature and not only of various urogenital malfunctions but of general complaints about declining physical or intellectual powers, proneness to 'spots' and other skin disorders etc. Sex education has lessened the cruder anxieties but by failing to point to the values of masturbation has left vague feelings of unease no doubt based on the earliest sexual prohibitions imposed by the parents.

Since it is a subject requiring attention in adolescent sex education some of the main points concerning masturbation are given :

(*a*) It is a universal activity from infancy to old age in man and the higher animals.

(*b*) It is no less normal in females than males and indeed is probably more frequently practised by them.

(*c*) Because of the greater sexual prohibitions culturally imposed on females and also because of their greater potential responsiveness to a large variety of stimuli, masturbation is not as easy to define or detect in them as the male and, unlike the male, signs of arousal and orgasm are easier to deny.

(*d*) In men (but much more so in women) varying degrees of self-deception about masturbation are possible but this is developmentally harmful since the individual is failing to accept his own sexuality fully, i.e. the condition is one of psychic castration which augurs badly for the future man/woman relationship. Indirect methods of masturbation are the product of a form of self-deception. Self-deception about sex involves dissociation at a conscious level between behaviour and intent or between action and gratification. Common examples in respect of masturbation are denial of pleasure and therefore, in a sense, the act or the suppression of conscious fantasy in masturbation or its replacement with apparently non-sexual material.

(*e*) Basically masturbation prepares the way for future efficiency in intercourse. The analogy between learning to talk and conversation is the same as that between masturbation and intercourse.

(*f*) Masturbation implies acceptance of one's own sexuality and through fantasy that of the opposite sex and their genitals. It therefore assists with the many changes to be made in the body image during adolescence and draws the body image of the opposite sex closer.

(*g*) Masturbation is used as a tension regulator by the young particularly—it tends, for example, to rise before exams—and it is only if it is used habitually to evade reality that it could be harmful.

(*h*) The fantasy component of masturbation, which becomes prominent first in pre-adolescence and early adolescence, is an important way in which the earlier attitudes towards the opposite sex are modified and contemporaries of the opposite sex start to be seen as objects to be desired and valued.

(*i*) Masturbation is an aspect of the personality and expresses something about it. In consequence active and intelligent people will tend to be active and intelligent in masturbation as well as other sexual activities.

(*j*) Some cases of psychotic illnesses are marked by disorders in masturbation but masturbation is never the direct cause of such illnesses. No disease either physical or psychical can directly result from masturbation as such, but only from guilt about it.

(*k*) Apart from (*j*) above the concept that any particular level of masturbation is 'excessive' is as ridiculous as to believe that walking more than a certain given distance is excessive. Individuals vary in their capacity for both experiences but there can be compulsive elements about the activity.

(*l*) Occasional 'perverse' fantasies in masturbation are no necessary indication of any disorder since many adolescents explore all the possibilities through fantasy and in practice are not found to come to any harm through it. On the other hand the fantasies can be of the greatest possible value in diagnosing and treating any sexual disorder that may be present. Some 'spread' of sexual interest is of value in the man/woman relationship since it permits more variety; and in the light of modern knowledge much less behaviour can now be regarded as 'perverse' than in the past.

(*m*) The vast majority of individuals, perhaps all, continue to masturbate at least occasionally after a perfectly satisfactory sexual relationship has been established. It is not a sign that the relationship is necessarily inadequate in any way.

(*n*) Excessive guilt over masturbation leads many adolescents to early intercourse as a refuge from the fears (including that of homosexuality) which masturbation inspires.

(*o*) Except in the immature with low tension tolerance masturbation does not replace the desire for intercourse.

Although the 'substitute' argument against masturbation is commonplace i.e. it is replacing normal intercourse which would be available to all from puberty onwards except for artificial social restraint, its acceptance seems to be a necessary precondition of later effectiveness in intercourse. The intervention of an intense auto-erotic stage in the second half of childhood i.e. adolescence, seems to have social and personal value as well as biological merit. Early pregnancy is avoided and personality development can proceed on a more even basis without an excessive preoccupation with heterosexual relations. It affords a breathing space in which adaptation to change can occur, and old love/sex objects are removed whilst new ones are endowed with value in their place.

Some complaints of impotence and frigidity in the young male derive entirely from the shame and guilt they have been made to feel about their own sexuality including masturbation. The psychosexual history is normal and even discussing it is curative. More serious problems arise where the history shows departures from normality and masturbation has never been fully accepted. These usually result from some serious trauma arising directly from the individual's own sexuality. Instances are legion. They are often hard to recover due to the repression to which the memory has been subjected. Sudden swift recollections often associated with blushing, tears and other evidences of the distress felt at the time the trauma occurred are produced with statements such as 'I never thought about it from that day to this'. Other episodes of suppression undoubtedly arose earlier but all the unconscious attention is devoted to the one occasion where the child has been exposed to intense fear, humiliation, physical pain, deprivation or shame over some act involving its sexuality. Common instances include vicious attacks on the child for masturbation (these being particularly serious if they occur about the time of puberty), for games involving undressing, or generally for any display of sexual interest. The individual thereafter has to deny his or her own sexuality.

In some cases so much fear is attached to genitality—or alternatively so much pleasure is attached to some other erotic area—that the patient remains fixed in, or reverts to, an earlier level of sexual gratification. In one convent-reared depressed, obese and frigid married patient, who also complained unreasonably about her slight hirsutism, a history of alcoholism and multiple drug addiction emerged, combined with erotic fantasies of men sucking large lactating breasts and conscious erotic arousal at the sight of cow's udders. Her favourite sexual act was fellatio, genital masturbation was rare and unsatisfactory and her intended profession was journalism. The mouth carried not only the burden of her sexuality but half her personality and ambition as well.

More complicated disorders arise where the sexuality, which in itself may seem to be normal, can only be expressed with others under particular conditions. Homosexuality, or rather fears of it, are commonplace amongst students and it is frequently referred to in jokes. Most queries about the subject are based on some misunderstanding such as the student's detection of characteristics of the opposite sex in themselves, but of the remainder, fear of sexual expression with the opposite sex is the basic underlying cause and this seems to be oedipal in origin. Amongst students simple reassurance here is useless. A detailed assessment must be made and the reasons given. A number of students are practising homosexuals and sometimes this is due arrest of psychosexual development in the homosexual phase in others the homosexual interest seems pervasive right through the sexuality and back to the psychosexual history. Even these can be 'cured' without recourse to elaborate techniques of treatment by insight, control over fantasy and generally supportive therapy but a good proportion default and thereafter happily accept their homosexual lot or become bisexual. Homosexuality is an example of those conditions where there is not necessarily any inhibition of personal sexuality—it is simply that its mode of expression towards others takes a form which earns social disapproval. Exhibitionism, sado-masochism, bestiality, peadophilia and so on, all of which arise in a student population, are, or may be, similar examples.

PROMISCUITY

Promiscuity is a good example of a condition which seems to be a sexual problem at first sight but is a symptom of an underlying emotional disturbance. Perhaps seven to ten per cent of students of both sexes are promiscuous but they have to be distinguished from the remainder of the population on some basis other than just the number of partners they have had. After all, everyone who is honest is at least potentially promiscuous and prone to flirting. Fear of rejection, shame about possible detection, dread of the possible consequences and, in men particularly, apprehensiveness about performance as well as loyalty to the established partner are the usual deterrents which keep most people in some sort of check. The promiscuous are not so deterred since, unlike the others, their main aim is not sexual. At a conscious level they don't much like sex, most such boys reporting a near dislike of women and intercourse and the girls usually being frigid and often fearful of men. Such a girl may really be seeking protective non-sexual (i.e. pregenital) love. Promiscuous males are ambivalent towards their mothers and one part of them seeks to humiliate and punish women, the majority of whom they regard with concealed contempt. Intercourse is often sought under degrading conditions. When such a student does fall in love he is usually impotent. Promiscuous girls are usually depressive and seek to distract the male from paying attention to their deeply felt physical and personality inadequacies by resorting to intercourse on short acquaintance and minimal prompting.

Inhibited girls can sometimes behave in a manner which seems identical with that of the promiscuous one but the psychodynamics are different. She has been made to feel so ashamed of her own sexuality that she is inhibited even with her own partner. It is as if she has been trained to believe that she will lose love and esteem if she shows her sexuality. However, under conditions, which she might seek, where she is not known and she will not meet the male again she feels able to reveal the full strength of her sexual impulses. Her aims are purely sexual and such occurrences are particularly likely to occur when abroad in the summer vacation. The inhibited of both sexes are likely to display impulsive sexual behaviour when they feel the restraints don't exist and they are often unaware of the deliberate but unconscious manner in which they create the right circumstances. Since denial of intent is involved precautions are not to hand so this type of behaviour is a common cause of the unwanted pregnancy. A general reduction in shame about sexual needs (which, of course, starts with parents) would eliminate silly behaviour of this type.

Students often seek advice about sexual matters with the unconscious aim of obtaining indirect 'permission' to indulge in sex. Thus a girl who talks to her tutor about her relationship with her boyfriend may well interpret a question about the closeness of the relationship as being a form of permission from a parent figure. All that can be done about this is to discuss the sexual aspects of life openly and where this mechanism seems to be operating make the student fully aware that the responsibility for their own behaviour is theirs. Constantly the advice should be given that if there is any danger of conception or high levels of guilt the act is best avoided. Conventional attitudes which tend to conceal sexual matters make it possible for the young to avoid a sense of personal responsibility.

UNWANTED PREGNANCY

Considered psychologically the unwanted pregnancy has multiple causes and is best regarded, amongst students, as a symptom of a psychosexual or personality disorder. Many causes are deliberate or near-deliberate no matter how unconscious the motivation. The common mechanisms lying behind it are denial of sexuality (due to shame) leading to self-deceit, depressiveness leading to the need for a dependent love object in the form of a baby, guilt requiring punishment, repetition neurosis due to a previous pregnancy or being born illegitimate, unconscious encouragement by the parents, escape from her course, neurotic attitudes towards love aimed at enslaving the other through a child, punishment of the parents or partner or self-dramatization. What at first sight appears to be ignorance or bad luck usually turns out to be the first cause listed above on closer scrutiny. Reliance on inefficient methods of contraception, especially by the inexperienced, is often based on sexual shame preventing a request being made for oral contraception and this failure is then rationalized on a self-deceiving notion such as 'I am not going to do it again'.

Complaints of symptoms when taking oral contraception spring from the same source but are often disguised as medical fears. Even if there are no complaints pills may be unaccountably missed (often on a visit to the parental home) or the course may be suddenly stopped on one pretext or another. A search for an underlying psychosexual disorder resulting in one or other of the dynamics listed above coming into play should be made and are usually found. Eradicating the shame, guilt or inhibition increases the patient's safety but this is not always easy to achieve. Moreover, it is not impossible that the few rare cases of real harm arising from the pill are due to, or are aggravated by, hormonal distresses secondary to emotional upsets connected with sex. In one case a student who had been well on the pill developed a thrombo-embolism a few hours after a sharp conflict with her mother who had discovered the pill. Menstrual disorders, for example, which are hormonally mediated can and do result from sexual activity. Thus fear of pregnancy, or rather guilt about exposure, can result in amenorrhoea (no periods) and an internal and unconscious conflict about whether she should have intercourse with her boy-friend can result in prolonged bleeding thus preventing the act that she consciously asserts she wishes to undertake.

It would now seem to be beyond question that most higher educational institutions are prepared to treat sexual matters as falling within the domain of private behaviour. It thus follows that adequate, confidential, widely publicized, and friendly contra-ceptive advice must be made available to students. From practical experience it was found that such a service combined with a good sex education programme will reduce the unwanted pregnancy rate by about half amongst students. A good programme is itself therapeutic for the milder cases of psychosexual disorders based on guilt and shame etc. but attendance can never be made com-pulsory. Probably those girls who are most likely to become un-wantedly pregnant are the ones least likely to attend because of the anxiety and shame such attendance might arouse. It is from this fraction, that is, the more seriously disturbed, that the unwantedly pregnant student is now recruited. Needless to say the unwanted pregnancy or even the fear of one is a marvellous opportunity for the practice of preventive medicine not only in the obvious sense of giving contraceptive advice but also of eliminating the underlying disorder thereby benefiting the individual in several ways at the same time. For this reason pregnancy testing of urine is a service which Student Health Services should offer.

5

Physical and Psychosomatic Illnesses

STUDENTS differ little from other adolescents in their physical illnesses and the group as a whole are the fittest in the community. Serious illness arises with sufficient frequency to prevent student health from becoming boring on this side but minor respiratory, dermatological, alimentary and gynaecological illnesses account for the bulk of this work with injuries and dental conditions being common. Requests for inoculations and vaccinations for travel purposes are large in volume and endless certificates and records of physical examinations are required for a surprising variety of purposes. Defects of hearing and vision need attention and hay-fever is troublesome due to the coincidence of the season with the pre-examination period.

However, physical illnesses are of importance in student health in a variety of ways. Firstly, they do establish contact between the service and the individual. They are sometimes used as a 'visiting card' by the student who has more serious problems he wishes to discuss. The encounter should be managed in a way that he has the fullest opportunity to talk if he wishes. Secondly, although the illness might not be psychosomatic in the usual sense of the word the student may have elected to report with that particular physical illness—as opposed to ignoring it or treating it himself—because of some special anxiety attached to the symptoms. Unless this is detected and handled he has not been fully treated. Thus a rash may become attached to fears of V.D. based on guilt about a recent sexual experience, but the anxiety may well not be revealed. Complaints of trivial conditions raise the suspicion that this type of motive is the underlying cause. In a similar way conditions involving minimal pain can seem to be unbearable to the depressed and a desire for some form of comforting attention can bring in students who are feeling isolated or who are regressing in the face of some fear with almost any complaint that readily comes to hand. Sometimes the particular symptoms may have some special significance for the student; for example, a cough may cause special alarm in someone whose father died of cancer of the lung.

The consequences of physical illness can raise special complications for students and normal therapeutic practices may require modification to overcome difficulties. The aims are to avoid interference with his capacity to work and to minimize absence from work as far as possible. Surgical operations, for example, are carried out in vacations whenever feasible i.e. they may be delayed; but any necessary hospital investigations of conditions preventing work through anxiety or other causes are carried out as promptly as circumstances allow. If a student has had to be admitted to hospital earlier than usual discharge may be arranged, under supervision from the Student Health Service, again to minimize time loss. Certain conditions, such as acne, may receive particularly thorough treatment where they are disturbing the body image excessively and interfering with interpersonal relationships to the detriment of work.

One illness which is often associated especially with students is glandular fever or infectious mononucleosis. It is sometimes called the 'kissing disease' because it is thought that it may be transmitted in this manner. Many cases are subclinical, that is, the individual is insufficiently troubled by his symptoms to report them or they are so mild and atypical that the condition is not diagnosed. At the other extreme the condition can, rarely, be very serious but most cases present with a sore throat, a headache, a temperature, enlarged glands and malaise but other presentations are common. Usually the student is fit enough to resume work in a week or two and some can continue throughout although restrictions on activity are necessary. The disease, however, can linger on for several months and be punctuated with exacerbations of the symptoms.

Just as physical symptoms can be over-laid with emotional reactions so emotional disturbances can be manifest in physical complaints or even physical signs. These are the psychosomatic diseases and they often first start under the stress of adolescence in the same way that the personality disorders, neuroses and psychoses often have their first manifestations in the period too. This is not unexpected.

The interactions between the psyche and the soma are complex. Not everyone who has an emotional disturbance, even a severe one, produces a psychosomatic or any other form of illness so other factors such as genetic predisposition, parental attitudes towards illness and the strength of the individual's ego in the face of outer or inner adversity, including attacks from an over-strong super-ego, are important too. In a family, for example, where consider-able attention is addressed to bowel function constipation may be a way of expressing emotional tension (such as a resentment against the demands being made by other members) which by some un-conscious rule within the family entitles the sufferer to special consideration. It is not difficult to imagine that a student from such a family will experience constipation when encountering difficulty. In fact it is remarkable how frequently with this type of complaint the student volunteers 'My mother/father/brother etc. have the same thing'. Menstrual disorders particularly follow this pattern.

Emotional factors are aetiologically important in another way. Accidents may be a way of escaping something worse and the depressed, or chronically tense are probably less likely to be able to overcome infections with germs causing respiratory disease than others and so proceed to a clinically manifest illness. Emotional disturbances have physiological effects and where the state is chronic structural changes may finally arise. This consideration may be of importance in some cases of heart disease, high blood pressure, peptic ulcer, some skin diseases, some glandular dis-turbances such as thyroid over-activity, and disorders of the large bowel (colon) amongst others. Tenseness in interpersonal relation-ships may, for example, be expressed in muscle tension or changes in the mucous lining of the nose and permanent changes may finally result in muscular 'rheumatism' or catarrh. Why one organ should be selected rather than another is unknown but it is note-worthy in students that 'curing' one psychosomatic illness can result in the precipitation of another unless the underlying emotional factors receive concomitant attention. Thus attacks of, say, asthma may give way to a skin disease and so on.

Since the skin is so intimately concerned with the body image it is a particular target organ in adolescence and seems to be usually linked to sexual guilt or shame. Thus one boy who had had a chronic erythematous (red) papular (raised) rash of the lower abdomen which had resisted all treatment over the years finally admitted that it had appeared within a day or two of his com-mencing adolescent masturbation. Without any further treatment it disappeared within forty-eight hours. In a girl psoriasis of the legs, lower trunk and arms first started within hours of the loss of her virginity (to a stranger in a foreign land and apparently on impulse) but it did not respond to psychotherapy; rather it waxed and waned in accordance with her sexual activity finally clearing up in the third year. In a similar way acne can wax and wane with the amount of guilt experienced about current sexual activity and in some cases serves to resolve a sexual conflict by making the student feel that he is so unattractive that it is not worthwhile attempting to do what he consciously says he wishes to do i.e. obtain a partner. So again psychosomatic conditions may provide an excuse which prevents something worse, such as the confirmation of rejectability, occurring. One girl regularly developed vulval warts, one each side of the introitus, whenever she actively contemplated intercourse with a specific individual and rashes, soreness and pains in an around the penis are common in those with sex guilt.

Blushing, an acute skin rash, is a related phenomenon of which students frequently complain and seek treatment. In one such case the blush was permanent and existed in the form of extensive red rash of the face which frequently became worse during therapy when certain topics were mentioned. It became apparent that the student had a phobia about speaking in a group of people, which was a disability of consequence on his course, and agarophobia. He had been reared in a children's home due to his mother's irregular life, and had been soundly thrashed by the woman in charge for looking at a naked girl on one occasion and looking in the direction of a woman in a bikini on another. He, to his utter humiliation, had been stripped nude in front of the girls to receive some medical treatment and his first 'offence' occurred after this episode. All his symptoms remitted when the story—and some other matters—had finally been revealed and untangled but it illustrates the emotional complexity that can underlie a case which first presented as a simple case of excessive shyness and timidity. The student's manifest personality changed considerably during treatment and he became much more confident, self-assertive and efficient. He even found his first girlfriend and became able to express aggressive feelings without guilt or excess.

Some psychosomatic complaints are only present at certain times—as would be expected—such as headaches and visual disturbances that commence with study, 'cystitis' that afflicts a girl on her visits to the parental home and abdominal uneasiness, even leading to vomiting, on dreaded social occasions. Students in difficulty often produce symptoms when travelling to the institution in the morning. In one case an urticarial rash appeared fairly often at 9 a.m. in a student with a very successful father.

Elements of self-punishment are to be found in psychosomatic illness. Good examples are seen in girls who are doubtfully embarking on advanced heterosexual activities. Such a student may be disturbed not only by sexual conflicts based on guilt but also by the acceptance of, and final identification with, her female role that her behaviour implies. This may be in conflict with her academic and other aims such as proving she is as good as her brother. In these cases 'cystitis' (i.e. painful and frequent urination sometimes containing blood) can be a frequent occurrence and can cause much more distress than the symptoms would seem to warrant. Often it is not due to any detectable infection nor to the mechanical irritation of 'honeymoon cystitis' since intercourse might not have occurred or is a rare event. It is presumably based on pelvic congestion (i.e. the physiological response to arousal unrelieved by orgasm) as is the pruritus vulvae (itching) which also commonly occurs in these cases. Menstrual disorders such as excessive pain or changes in flow by way of excess or deficiency often accompanied by increases in vaginal secretion are all common and lead to fears of V.D. or pregnancy or of internal disorder and injury. In one case the patient started her period early following extra-marital intercourse and presented urgently with intense fears that she was dying from heart disease (which had special significance for her) or leukaemia. In this way she both distracted herself from her real anxiety which was moral guilt and severely punished herself at the same time.

The punishment of others i.e. concealed aggression also is a motive of importance in some psychosomatic conditions. In anorexia nervosa, which occurs in students often under the veil of dieting, there is usually a great deal of hostility in the girl towards her mother who probably rejected her in part. Food is rejected either directly or through vomiting and weight is lost, the periods cease and the breasts disappear. As a student the girl is almost always alert, very intelligent and able but is usually resistant to treatment. Practical interest in sex is negligible but most cases have an attractive neatness of appearance, work and behaviour. Rejection of the female role or adult sexuality may be important and there is a certain emotional immaturity expressed in the form of attitudes reminiscent of the little girl evident in them. Rejecting food may be a way of rejecting the mother and she normally responds with greater anxiety which is not altogether misplaced since death can occur and is really a form of suicide. Rejecting the female form and role may be another way of rejecting and punishing the mother.

Migraine is possibly a psychosomatic disease which can have catastrophic effects on exam performance if an attack occurs at this time. Emotional stress often seems to precipitate an attack and those who suffer from the condition may be inadequate at expressing hostility and aggression in a more direct form. Although any severe headache is likely to be labelled migraine, in the medical condition so named paroxysmal headache, visual and abdominal symptoms usually occur. The attack can be disabling and last for the best part of a day or even two.

Some doctors are sceptical about diagnoses which involve psychosomatic factors but it is to be doubted that anyone working in student health would join them in their views. The factors which most lend conviction to such a diagnosis is the demonstration of underlying emotional—as opposed to physical—pathology and the remission of signs and symptoms which occur when this receives attention. A psychosomatic component may be present in all illnesses no matter how 'physical' they appear and it may be one of the factors which explain why a particular individual contracts a particular disease when others equally exposed or likely to suffer from it do not. The manifestations of psychosomatic illness, at least in students, can mimic those of almost all 'physical' diseases but in many instances the signs and symptoms are bizarre and merge into those due to hysteria. Students often resent, initially, the suggestion that their troubles are psychosomatic in origin believing that this is equivalent to dismissing their complaints out of hand. However, as demonstrated above many of the conditions are serious and nearly all of them are complex. Viewed in one way they all look like inefficient and immature methods of coping with emotional disturbances but, also, they are all in some degree protective and resolve problems arising from intrapersonal or interpersonal relationships.

One aspect of psychosomatic medicine is therapeutic and concerns the placebo response. In this condition pharmacologically inert substances exert a beneficial effect on symptoms since the patient has the prior expectation that they will do so. Although opinions on the point vary on the whole it is better not to rely on the placebo response in students since they are astute at discovering and then looking up the nature of substances prescribed. It is better either to prescribe nothing or effective remedies since a reputation for any form of chicanery is most undesirable.

A phenomenon related to psychosomatic medicine is hypochondriasis and this is common in adolescents in general and students in particular. In the interests of posture, control and self preservation the body possesses a monitoring system which relays information about its functions to the central nervous system. Normally these messages pass largely unnoticed by the conscious mind but the means exist to bring matters to attention where necessary. Thus a sudden pain will focus the faculties on determining the source and nature of the pain with the object of taking remedial action if possible e.g. removing the hand from a very hot surface. Such an experience creates a certain amount of fear and tension which is usually discharged in an irritable curse or even an attack on the source of the discomfort.

In the hypochondriac the source of the ordinary internal body messages are constantly presented to the conscious mind and/or the dreaming mind for attention. The resultant preoccupation is a neurotic over-concern for the physical aspects of the self. Sometimes illness in the self or in others known to the patient starts the process going but often, and commonly in students, the physiological consequences of anxiety or depression are themselves the starting point. Sometimes secondary gain is obvious and the picture again verges into hysteria but in other cases there is a conviction of underlying illness with a history of having consulted many doctors, undergone many hospital investigations and even operations. Operations are sometimes much desired and seem to prove to the patient that he is really ill. Symptoms continue after operation. Resistance to psychological exploration is usually suspiciously strong. Orthopaedic complaints often fall into this category in students. In some cases the aim seems not to evade some unpleasant situation, such as exams, but rather to obtain admiration from tutors, parents and friends for the bravery and stoicism displayed by enduring both exams and painful conditions. Presumably too, if one should fail, although these students never do, a ready-made excuse to the self and others exists. At a simpler and more normal level bandages and plasters play a similar role after small injuries. They entitle the wearer to consideration and commiseration.

4—SH　*　*

It is easy to see that failures or those who unduly fear failure, such as some mature students, may develop hypochondriacal symptoms to account for their inadequacy in a more acceptable way than simple want of ability but it is less obvious that underlying such symptoms may lurk the expectation or desire for punishment to expiate guilt. Symptoms arising from oral contraception are mostly of this type. This keeps the symptoms going, constitutes a form of punishment in itself and may help the super-ego to keep the instinctual forces in check by a threat that asserts the symptoms are only the harbingers of a serious, and possibly fatal, illness which will later befall the individual unless he behaves himself. Hypochondriacs often have rigid personalities of this type. Since the adolescent is struggling to control instinctual forces this might account for the severity of some cases of hypochondriasis in students and the extreme panic attacks which arise in conjunction with them. The irrational and neurotic force behind their symptoms often makes these patients hard to treat where the symptomatology is well established but in the early cases incipient adolescent hypochondriasis can be 'nipped in the bud' with some ease if the underlying pathology receives attention. In these cases, as in others, the student's initial disbelief turns into acute interest which overcomes the symptoms and their cause through insight. Amusement replaces anxiety and all is well again. Personality development can then proceed.

Doctors can induce adolescent hypochondriasis and in one extreme case a healthy student from the Middle East had been admitted to an oil company's underemployed and over-equipped hospital for ten days with tonsillitis and was maintained continuously on an E.C.G. machine. Subsequently, he was intensely conscious of cardiac activity—which in itself disturbs such activity due to anxiety—and reported continuously with pains and disturbances of consciousness which heralded, he felt, impending doom. He was cured only with great difficulty. Some doctors, too, are hostile to all but serious illness in adolescents and tend to treat the student's concern about himself with scorn. However, no matter what the blend of physical, psychosomatic or psychological illness the student who takes the trouble to consult a doctor is always a student in some degree of difficulty.

6

Anxiety and Depression

ANXIETY and depression are a complex couple. As seen in students they almost always occur together in variable proportions. Both lie well within the range of the normal everyday experience of everyone, and anyone who reports the absence of such feelings is either denying them as a defence against them or is abnormal in some way. Within limits society tolerates and even expects both reactions to occur in certain circumstances. Anxiety in the face of some physical danger is considered normal and its absence the sign of a brave man or a fool. Depression on bereavement is expected and its absence earns condemnation. Women and children are permitted to display more of both reactions with less provocation than men. Inside the limits set there is an area of choice and the amount of reaction shown is ascribed to the personality of the individual. Someone who shows less than average anxiety in given circumstances is regarded as possessing 'cool nerves' whereas someone who is prone to react with depression to some trifling adversity is 'easily got down'.

Both reactions can result from events in either the external or the internal environment. Being confronted with a lion (in the form, perhaps, of one's professor) or the loss of one's job (by failing exams, for instance) may reasonably be expected to result in anxiety and depression respectively. However, the fear that one might be confronted with a lion or lose one's job can also provoke the same reactions. Most people are sufficiently realistic to know that life is going to produce danger and adversity but are not too preoccupied with the possibilities until they actually exist. Others, though, for reasons which are inborn or the product of rearing experience are particularly prone to anticipate, consciously or unconsciously, the possibilities and elevate them to near certainties. Removing one source of worry, merely leads to the institution of others. Yet other people over-react in general to actual or possible sources of anxiety or depression to an above average degree and so are 'neurotic' in disposition. Due to special conscious or unconscious associations other people vastly over-react to a limited number of such stimuli and in the case of anxiety are said to be public. In the case of depression it is postulated by some psychiatrists that it can descend out of the blue for reasons to do with brain chemistry.

In addition to the internal mental processes of imagination and foresight which make apprehensions about future possible events sources of anxiety and depression, other sources exist which are related to previous experiences. If an individual has been reared to suppress manifestations of love, aggression or sexuality etc. then the fact that under certain circumstances or at certain times they are seeking expression leads to anxiety. The anxiety is mainly the anxiety the individual was made to feel when the suppression was originally imposed on him. If, in spite of anxiety, these needs are expressed then the individual may hate himself for it and thereby be depressed. These are distressing events for which some solution is sought.

Obviously anxiety and depression have survival value for the species since in addition to making it possible for the child to be socialized they offer a means whereby threats to existence can be dealt with or avoided. Depression may be particularly associated in some way with love (see below) and love certainly has survival value for the individual and the species. A capacity to be anxious is obviously inborn and certain anxieties are routinely experienced. Early experiences associated with anxiety might determine the form, extent and strength of the anxiety attending anxiety-provoking circumstances in the future. A similar statement might also be true of depression. Routine anxiety presumably accompanies birth and subsequently thirst and hunger. Relief of the physical needs of thirst and hunger show all the signs of pleasure whereas non-satisfaction leads to evidence of mounting anxiety culminating in rage at the frustration and this may be followed by apathy. Other anxieties attend separation from parents—which every child must learn to withstand—threats of physical punishment or withdrawal of love.

Suppression of sexual acts leads to anxiety about sex and when the child is involved in the oedipal situation the anxiety comes to the fore since the stage is a sexual one. The anxiety may be general but it also takes a specific form which in boys is to do with the revenge he thinks his father might seek for him thinking of the father as a rival of whom the boy wishes to be rid. This is castration (of the penis) anxiety. This illustrates an important point. There are elements in anxiety which determine the form in which it is expressed and these have contemporary significance. Thus the little girl who was made over-anxious about her sexuality has fears of pregnancy as an early adolescent when she first kisses a boy and of V.D. when she first undertakes intercourse. These fears may not be regarded as altogether unreasonable but in some girls they cause enormous emotional upheavals amounting to phobias. Some of the fears that adolescent boys have of women and intercourse derive directly from castration anxiety and are simply updated. Thus fears of harm or of doing harm, of V.D., of failure to erect, or of penile inadequacy are related to original castration anxiety and if this was strong then subsequent derived anxieties will be strong to an irrational degree. Earlier forms of anxiety may persist as husks but are not usually invested with any emotional force. In cases where they do persist neuroses may develop.

Depression may be underlaid by similar mechanisms. Both anxiety and depression say something about the individual, his experiences, his family and the society in which they live. Not only may the form of both be determined by such experiences but also the level at which they are experienced. Apprehensive and fearful parents produce anxious children. Since anxiety tends to have visible consequences and affect others it may be more easily transmitted than depression.

Various ways of coping with anxiety and depression have been mentioned earlier but by way of generalization it can be observed in practice that the sufferer uses one or more of the following techniques :

(a) The real source of the anxiety or the depression is acknowledged and attempts are made to deal with it.

(b) The real source is not acknowledged, presumably because it is too painful, but some other more acceptable substitute stands in place of it. For example, a student who is unbearably anxious about impending examinations may believe that its real origin is a concern about the health of a parent who in fact is suffering only from some trifling disability.

(c) The anxiety or depression is denied since what doesn't exist can't be acknowledged and neither can its cause. Its presence may then be manifested in behavioural forms (i.e. acting-out) or in disturbances of function (e.g. depersonalization, refuge in sleep or purposeless over-activity).

(d) The feelings of anxiety or depression are detached from their source in order that the origin can be denied. The feelings remain but the cause is unknown so the emotion is free floating.

(e) The feelings are somatized and thereby find psychosomatic expression which deprives them of the ability to upset emotional equilibrium. Alternatively it could be postulated that the mechanism is the same as in (b) above and the individual prefers to worry about the illness rather than the source of the anxiety or the depression.

(f) The tension engendered by the feelings is expressed in the form of a personality or psychosexual disorder including hypochondriasis. In students, at least, these can be fleeting rather than permanent.

The eternal problem for the doctor is to decide when anxiety or depression require treatment. One answer is that it is necessary when any but the first solution above is used to deal with the situation. Another is when they begin to impair to a significant degree the capacity for work, leisure or interpersonal relations. Since this depends upon the situation of the individual, treatment would start a good deal earlier in a student than in a bricklayer as far as the criteria of work is used since anxiety and depression interfere with intellectual work long before they significantly reduce physical capacities. A third answer is to treat any patient who complains and this is not unreasonable provided it is acknowledged that the underlying factors may also need attention if the condition does not quickly resolve itself. Treatment may tide the patient over until the sources of the anxiety or the depression have passed but where they are chronic some form of psychotherapy or other treatment may be necessary. At the moment more effective therapeutic techniques exist for dealing in the long term with depression than anxiety but the reverse is true on short term considerations.

ANXIETY

Anxiety is an unpleasant emotion, which might be welcome to some people, arising when some danger of either internal or external origin is perceived or apprehended, falsely or otherwise, which threatens the physical or psychic welfare of the self or of others who are of concern. Medical reports on students often refer to anxiety but the terminology is very confusing indeed. Individuals who perceive or apprehend danger in nearly everything may be described as possessing timid or anxious personalities or as being anxiety prone. Individuals who perpetually over-react to small stimuli may be said to be neurotic in character. Those who display the signs and symptoms of anxiety in either acute or chronic form for no readily apparent reason suffer from an anxiety state. People who display the symptoms and signs of an acute anxiety state in response to some specific and personal stimulus peculiar to them are phobic. Anyone in a severe state of acute anxiety is in a panic. Individuals who suffer from an anxiety neurosis are usually in a more or less chronic anxiety state, perhaps punctuated with attacks of acute anxiety but in some of the other neuroses (page 106) the element of anxiety is not very prominent although other symptoms (which are defences) are in the foreground. A person who experiences anxiety to an appropriate degree in the presence of appropriate stimuli, much like anyone else, is simply said to be anxious. All these states are encountered in students. Some students cannot tolerate the anxieties that are involved in being a student and unless this can be overcome by treatment the student should consider pursuing some career where examinations and similar stresses do not arise.

Anxiety has inborn, learned, cultural and personal components, and can be induced by real or imagined dangers in the environment, by inner sensation such as choking or noticing an irregularity in the heart's action, by inner psychic threats, or by thoughts, fantasies, dreams and portrayals of tense situations in books, films and so on. Anxiety, with some attendant degree of depression, may exist on its own or in conjunction with additional psychic or physical symptoms or it may mask underlying serious illness or fear of it. Anxiety and depression are common reactions to the onset of any illness.

The symptoms and signs of anxiety vary from mild apprehension to extreme panic and include irritability, over-activity such as hand-wringing or pacing about (an anxious student will often ask to be excused from sitting down), or the paralysed terror of abject fear, excessive vigilance or preoccupation with inner thoughts i.e. normal attention is disturbed, crying and demands for reassurance, pallor and perspiration or flushing and anger; muscular tension, dizziness, loss of appetite, nausea and vomiting; tightness in the chest and rapid heartbeat, weakness and trembling, panting respiration, abnormal sensations in the hands, and headache; sensations of impending danger, frequent excretion, screaming and moaning; raised blood pressure, nose bleeding, insomnia and lassitude; feelings of depersonalization and derealization; fears of fainting, dying or going mad; frightening dreams often of inability to escape from some dangerous situation, disturbed sleep and so on. In anxiety states, acute attacks may last a few minutes to a few days but in the chronic form they can continue for months and years.

Medical reports to examiners about anxiety states arising in students in connection with examinations can seem like exaggerated pleas but no certificate can convey the extreme distress which can be witnessed in student health as the personality of the adolescent disintegrates and he turns into an absolutely terrified and helpless small, sobbing child bereft of all ability to think or take purposive action. Even in the armed services and in conditions where men succumb to their terrors of being destroyed one only rarely sees the extreme reactions which occur daily in student health work. It is the ongoing nature of the many stresses to which he is subject and the high sum of total stress which accounts for the apparently low thresholds seen in many students. Almost any trivial straw may be the last that they can bear and so release the acute anxiety state. Thus, an inability to recall one fact in a three hour written paper may precipitate an exam room breakdown but in the days and weeks beforehand his condition has been one of increasing fragility.

Anxiety levels may be high during novel experiences and since the student is so often in this situation it explains the high anxiety rates and 'neurotic' attitudes which are so frequently encountered in student health work. Habituation normally leads to a reduction in anxiety level but in some students the reverse is the case perhaps due to some personality factor. However, most students can be taught to increase their tolerance for anxiety by various techniques, such as discussion, direction of behaviour or fantasy, or the use of anxiety-relieving drugs, and some whose personalities can only be described as having been 'compressed' by criticism and other anxiety provoking experiences in the past can blossom out. Excessive anxiety can lead to thought-blocking in students and this can be disastrous in the exam room. Postgraduate students and those undergraduates on courses where initiative is required can reach a stage of work paralysis due to the anxiety they experience in making a move in any direction which might be criticized. Changes in circumstances generally may lead to anxiety since not only are the new circumstances novel but old mechanisms (i.e. defences) for coping may be inadequate. A previous adequacy can turn into inadequacy on leaving home, on getting married, on first entering into higher education and so on. Moderate or high levels of anxiety create a sense of tension which can be discharged through activity and this stresses the importance of adequate sporting and exercise facilities for students which, in some forms, should be available through the day and night. The original function of anxiety was probably to provide a signal to the individual that action needed to be undertaken.

Anxiety provoking situations are often welcomed by some students in order that they may assert mastery over their own fears or show off. Anxiety attending sexual activity can be pleasantly arousing and, conversely, anxiety can result in sexual arousal. It has been suggested that procrastination over work can be a form of masturbation in students (Blos). Security and ordered living can suddenly become boring to the student who then may develop desires to live dangerously. Fortunately, most of these impulses are probably accommodated by the cinema or television but participation in student demonstrations may also result.

In spite of the pleasurable aspects of anxiety there is a basic desire to run away in all forms of anxiety. Daydreams of vacations in sunny places become intensely appealing before exams. Some students do literally run away but for most this would create a secondary shame anxiety so strategies of retreat may be devisedf. whereby intention is concealed—at least from the student himself.

A similar concealment of motive occurs in the phobias. The commonest encountered in students are agarophobia, exam phobia, social phobias concerning blushing, eating or drinking in the presence of others, V.D. and other sex-based phobias, and heart phobias. In the sense that there is no underlying physical pathology they are akin to hysterical symptoms. One of two apparently contradictory techniques are often used in student health work to treat phobias. One depends on gradual exposure to the fear, usually through fantasy, combined with relaxation, whereas the other confronts the patient, again through fantasy, with his worst fears. The first is called desensitization and the second inplosion.

NEUROSES

The neuroses may consist of states where the predominant feature is anxiety itself when it is referred to as anxiety neurosis or anxiety state. The anxiety is generally free floating or its true source is not perceived. Where the anxiety is attached to a specific object or situation the class of neurosis is a phobia. Where the clinical picture is dominated not by anxiety symptoms but by symptoms leading to reduced use of a part of the body for which no physical cause can be found the type of neurosis is hysteria. If thinking and behaviour are disturbed by obsessional thoughts and compulsions to undertake certain actions the patient has an obsessional neurosis. The phobias, hysteria and obsessional neuroses are known as psychoneuroses. All are mechanisms or techniques for dealing with or defending against inner anxieties. The neuroses are the special province of the psychoanalysts who through their work with these patients, have shed much light on our understanding of the non-physical diseases to which students, particularly, are prone. It is far from necessary to use the insights they afford in every case of anxiety—if only because many cases are based mainly or wholly on real threats—but where the nature of the case or the past history so indicate their utilization makes further therapeutic progress possible. Techniques of treatment derived from psychoanalysis such as brief psychotherapy are of the utmost value. Students with neuroses, as opposed to those with simple anxiety, know that tablets will do them no permanent good and yearn to understand themselves. Psychotherapy is welcome to this group.

DEPRESSION

Depression is probably commoner than anxiety in a student population and in its more severe forms it is a disturbing and demoralizing condition, the onset of which is regarded with dread by students who have suffered previously. All cases have a potential for at least attempting suicide.

Depression seems to be analagous to anxiety and to have some intimate connection with it. Thus attacks of depression occur in response to a variety of situations which vary from real events in the outer environment to inner and obscure psychic processes which are related to past experience and attitudes towards the self. Sometimes the inner distress affects personality development so that the individual is depressive but does not necessarily have much depression. Attacks of depression may be acute or chronic. Some people react with depression to small stimuli whereas others can cope with large amounts of adversity and rarely suffer from much depression. Cultural factors affect depression and in some societies death, for example, is a matter for rejoicing. Constitutional factors are also involved and some people may have a greater proneness to depression for this reason alone. The physiological reactions which accompany anxiety and depression are perhaps related too. In ordinary physiological arousal in preparation for effort such as 'fight or flight' some systems like the gastro-intestinal tract reduce their activity in order to make supplies of blood available to the rest of the body whereas the heart, lungs and muscles increase their activity in order to anticipate the demand for effort. In anxiety the last group of changes occur and in depression the former.

It is of interest too that amongst students it can be seen that the same stimulus may result in either anxiety or depression (or rather both in some ratio). Quite a trivial episode in itself, such as being omitted from a party of friends going to the pub for a drink, can precipitate either reaction. Once started such a process may soon cease but can also be nourished by attention to the environment for other signs which are then interpreted as confirming to the student that he was right to be anxious about his status within the group or as supporting his belief that no one likes him and he is unworthy. Exams also can produce either reaction as can a poor mark for course work or a critical comment from a tutor. Critical attitudes towards the body image may evoke either anxiety or depression. Some students when separated from their opposite sex partner, for example, can display a lot of anxiety or depression which sometimes persists. The difference between the two states seems to be one of expectation. In the former there are underlying fears that the partner might find someone else they prefer during the absence whereas in the second there is the belief that this is inevitable eventually anyway due to faults lying within the depressed person himself.

Thus one difference between the two states, apart from the symptoms and feelings attached to them, may be anticipation based on prior experience starting, in the above case, with separation anxiety in early childhood. Another involves attitudes towards the self. In depression these are nearly always critical, hostile or despairing. There is a loss of self-respect, self-esteem and self-love. When depression starts (or is precipitated) as a result of events in the external environment there is always an element of not being good enough, not being liked, being left or abandoned and generally not being loved, about the situation. Even when the depression comes from within there is still the same self-devaluation and sense of unworthiness as if the individual had been judged and found wanting by another person whose love or regard was then withdrawn. (Presumably, 'the other' is the super-ego). The depressed person seeks to possess a sense of having been rejected or spurned. The self-reproaches often bear very little relation to reality.

This statement about depression may be over-coloured since it is essentially derived from students but in summary form it can be said that from working with them it seems that whereas the depressive feels basically and secretly unloveable the depressed person feels unloved. Depression is bound up with love and the development of love just as anxiety is the product of a real or imaginary threat to physical or psychic security. Since love and security are an intimately related couple it must be at this level, the one of early childhood, that anxiety and depression first associate.

Disposition, circumstances, experience and the family environment must decide whether and to what extent they will be present in future behaviour, at what threshold and in what situations they will be released, whether they will affect personality formation and the form or forms they will take. The complexity and variability of expression of anxiety and depression in later life reflect the complexities of the processes of maturation and the variability of personal experience. This explains why reassurance doesn't necessarily cure anxiety nor does love cure depression.

A third difference between the two is that whereas anxiety seems to provoke activity, or the desire for it, in order to deal with the threat or run away from it, there is a defeatism about depression which undermines work even more seriously than anxiety. The feelings of despair, the belief that no action could possibly help therefore all action is pointless is always present in depression but since anxiety and depression are mixed the depressed student may be over-active and the anxious may be paralysed. In anxiety the view is forward-looking and anticipatory but in depression the past is reviewed. However, anxious people may look backwards to justify their fears and depressed ones may look forward as if to affirm their gloomy prognostications.

Like anxiety depression can be evoked by thoughts, dreams, fantasies and books or films. Like anxiety some people find depression pleasurable and may even deliberately expose themselves to circumstances which can provoke it. The picture then looks like one of aggression, if only against self, and a non-sexual but masochistic desire for punishment. Some depressed students show high degrees of resentment and anger sometimes manifested in the form of fantasies in which others are made to feel sorry for their past behaviour towards the patient. Viewed like this all manner of behaviour such as excessive drinking, reckless driving, over-smoking, drug taking, some dangerous sports, walking out of exams, anorexia, taking sexual risks, some delinquency, and so on begin to look even more sinister than they do at first sight and raise questions about the possibility that they are behavioural expressions of depression, at least in some cases.

The terminology used to describe depression is again very confusing and medical reports need interpretation. Psychiatrists distinguish between reactive or neurotic or exogenous or psychoneurotic depression or depressive reaction and endogenous or psychotic depression. The manifestations are held to be very similar, if not indistinguishable, but the latter is regarded as being more serious than the first, probably requiring more thorough treatment. The presumption is that the first type of depression is a response, albeit excessive, to some cause in the environment whereas the second is the product of a constitutional (biological) disturbance which may be, some think, chemical in nature (a deficiency of mono-amines in the brain). Endogenous depression is regarded as psychotic since it is likely to be associated with delusions, hallucinations and loss of reality and some psychiatrists would not make the diagnosis in the absence of such symptoms but others would attach the title to any severe depression. Some believe that endogenous depression may express itself simply in symptoms of depression when they may refer to it as unipolar depression but others believe that attacks alternate with moods of mania, no matter how slight and no matter how long after the depression they occur, and so would not diagnose psychotic depression without a history suggestive of mood swings from sadness to elation. In consequence they label an attack of such depression as manic-depression or manic depressive psychosis or bipolar depression.

Individuals with the cyclothymic personality disorder are prone to have attacks of manic depression.

By definition environmental circumstances do not precipitate an attack of endogenous depression but it is thought that they might be related to its onset in some way. Some psychiatrists do not agree that there are two different forms of depression and believe there is only one which occurs with varying degrees of severity but those who believe in endogenous depression think that its course is longer, that it responds to different treatment and that in some ways its symptoms are different from those of reactive depression. Most doctors in student health would, I think, adopt the view that there is only one form of depression or alternatively that if true endogenous (as opposed to severe) depression exists it is rarely encountered in students today. However, students tend to somatize their psychic illnesses so a bout of psychosomatic illness followed by a spell of, say, reckless driving or even excessive and fairly superficial mental activity could be the mode of presentation of manic depression.

Attacks of depression last from a few hours to months and the longer they exist before treatment the harder they are to treat. However, spontaneous recovery is the rule amongst students so many cases do not come to notice but all who do, require treatment since it is difficult to foretell which course any particular case may follow. Once he has gained a consultation he may feel ashamed and make light of his symptoms or deny his depression. He usually looks pale and worn and tears may not be far away. Smiling is infrequent or absent and there is a sad, fixed look about the face and eyes. Speech is usually slow and may peter out in mid-sentence giving the impression that some sorrowful inner preoccupation of the mind is receiving attention rather than the consultation. Characteristically there is a reduction in movement and an economy of effort but this may be interspersed with bouts of agitated activity. The story usually starts with some account seeming to indicate a sense of isolation, difference and rejection by one or more other people with fears of being disliked leading on to accusations against himself for being what he is or what he has done in the past which abundantly justifies others in their opinions. After the manner of children the head may be held in the hands as if the face and its expression is not to be seen. This may happen as crying starts. A sort of sulky irresponsiveness may be present. When describing how he feels it is evident that all pleasure and hope have gone out of life; that nothing pleases and that the world has contracted down to his immediate environment or just his own mind. Some students mention an accompanying feeling of boredom along with wishes to escape (perhaps more from people than circumstances) and say that they are irritable if anyone should interfere with them. Since no one cares for him he may feel he cares for nothing and no one, but students moving into depression will sometimes establish contact with an animal or even acquire one of their own. They may also purchase some long wanted article that they can't afford. In his dejection he may attribute his past academic successes to hard work or a sheer fluke and claim he is stupid. Complaints about physical appearance are common and the self-denigration may also involve statements about the unattractiveness of his personality. If the trouble has arisen from a love affair he will heap all the blame on himself and blame himself for all sorts of other things as well. His sexual behaviour might well come in for attack. He may be regressed and want to be treated as a child or treat himself as one which might account for the spasms of increased eating found in depressed girls particularly. They may gain weight but there are times when interest in food is lost and this is typical of depression; a good deal of weight may be lost very rapidly. In depression interest in sex is lost but in the early stages of mild cases masturbation frequently increases in students presumably as a self-comforting (and self-loving) device or in an attempt to control tension. This seems to be especially true of women. When and if it ceases the case has become severe. Apathy and apathetic attitudes towards work, the future, interesting activities and the opposite sex are characteristic but in a minority of depressed students there is a desire to interact with people which might be undertaken on a frantic basis and may, in the case of girls, involve casual intercourse. After this early phase in which the intention is to shake off the impending attack the depression may sharply worsen. Suicidal thoughts are the rule and plans may be thought out and the means obtained. Just as appetite changes are variable so is sleep. Some depressed students not only sleep but oversleep and take refuge in sleep. Some can't get off to sleep but others retreat into sleep wherever possible. Sleep may or may not be disturbed and in some, waking in the early morning with or without gloomy thoughts occurs. Some depressed students manage to get moving only with enormous effort in the mornings whereas others start off well but as the day progresses wish more and more to reach the solitude of their own room—away from people. In consequence lectures are missed and this adds a component of anxiety or increases the sense of hopelessness.

Various somatic complaints may overlay the picture and may reflect both the needs for dependency and the fears of body malfunction. The picture varies in all degrees of severity and symptoms of anxiety are present as well.

SUICIDE

Suicide, or attempts thereat, are more common when an attack of depression is starting or finishing, before the will is lost or as it is regained. In the general population half of all suicides are associated with depression but amongst students the proportion is much higher. The same element of aggression directed against the self rather than being openly expressed against others is found in both suicide and depression. Suicide is commoner in men than women and the converse is true for attempted suicide. Attempted suicide is very much commoner than suicide amongst the young as opposed to the elderly. Suicide is commoner amongst students than comparable non-students and the same statement is almost undoubtedly true of attempted suicide but the extent to which this is so varies in different institutions. In one study of suicide in male ex-students of two U.S. universities it was found that early loss or absence of the father was the dominant distinguishing characteristic. Alcoholics and the children of alcoholic parents are more likely to commit or attempt suicide. Children from broken homes are also more vulnerable.

Suicides and attempted suicide occur not only in depressed people but in others who are in some sort of a crisis, particularly where personal or domestic problems appear or close personal bonds have been disrupted. Such events may be more frequent in the lives of individuals with hysterical or obsessive personality disorders and may account for their greater vulnerability to suicide.

The act or attempt may be impulsive but most cases (about seventy per cent) give some sort of prior notice of intent to doctors or friends. Such 'notices' are frequently received but only a minority are carried out. However, the student giving the notice is seriously thinking, rather than simply speculating, of resort to suicide as an escape or to attempted suicide as a means of altering his circumstances in some way. An attempt at suicide before exams may reflect a genuine effort to escape the examination or the consequences of the failure that is expected to follow through death or it may serve simply to avoid the examinations and gain some sympathy. It is very hard to estimate the proportions of serious intent, desire to influence others and the area left to chance. For example, the girl who takes two sleeping tablets sounds like a trivial attempt at a suicidal gesture aimed, perhaps, at ensuring due weight will be given to her troubles which she might think would not otherwise justify the attention of her tutor or doctor. It may be her way of adding emphasis to her complaints or of requesting help. However, when it is discovered that she really does believe that if one of the particular tablets involved makes you sleep all night then two may result in permanent sleep the situation is much more serious. Similarly, it is difficult to know how to assess claims by the student that he is habitually stepping into the road without looking. Thus it is important not only to know what the individual does but what he believes the outcome is likely to be. Most students attempting suicide do so by taking medicinal drugs, usually prescribed to treat anxiety and depression, but often they are only vaguely aware of the effects of over-dosage with these particular preparations. In consequence the method is often no reliable guide to intent. After an attempt which seems serious students are often ashamed and confused about their motives.

Where routine enquiries are made about thoughts of suicide something like four out of five students claim to have considered the possibility seriously at some time or another. Since this is so universal enquiring about suicidal thoughts is not likely, as some fear, to put the student in mind of it. A proportion of the girls, say about one in ten, will have a history of some form of attempt usually in mid-adolescence over a family quarrel or a boyfriend. Where there is a close family history of suicide the possibilities prey more heavily on the student's mind as those of insanity do in students who have such a family history.

The only effective course to follow is to regard all 'notices' and gestures or attempts as serious. The answer is not to send the student to a mental hospital or inform his parents but to commence effective therapy at once enlisting the aid of those about him if possible. Drug treatment is prescribed in small quantities for obvious reasons and also to bring the student back at frequent intervals. After assessing the nature of any crisis steps can be taken to resolve it either directly or through the student with the help of the tutor if the student gives consent. Even simple steps like providing a telephone number for him to ring at any time should he feel a recurrence of suicidal urges and extracting 'promises' can assist especially where the problems are neurotic in character. Those who show from their history or psychiatric assessment. that they are especially prone may need urgent psychiatric treatment perhaps as an in-patient. Adequate and effective supporting services are essential if the suicide rate is to be kept low or even eliminated : the student suicide rate is now declining. Suicidal gestures and attempt are always a sign of a student in difficulty.

7

Psychiatric Illnesses

MOST student health services aim at a high standard of psychiatric efficiency and may have part-time, or even full-time, psychiatrists on their staff. About a tenth of all consultations in student health work are for psychological illnesses of the types discussed earlier. About fifteen to thirty per cent of all students will seek such help and about one per cent or less will be referred to a psychiatrist. Some of these will be suffering from psychoses.

Some students welcome reference to a psychiatrist, they may even demand it, but most are reluctant or very reluctant. Where the psychiatrist is on the health service staff and is known to the students this difficulty is overcome. For many students and even more, their parents, seeing a psychiatrist is synonymous with being mad. Unless the student has to be urgently admitted for a serious psychiatric condition it is almost pointless forcing him to attend since he is likely to be resentful and unhelpful. It may even adversely affect him and his attitudes towards the Student Health Service. Girls are more likely to attend willingly than boys. Harm can be done in another way since admission to a psychiatric institution can lead to the acquisition of symptoms from other patients. Some students will see a psychiatrist once and then stead-fastly refuse to keep further appointments. Psychiatry is a topic of interest to many students but psychiatrists, on the whole, have a bad reputation which is made worse by the mass media and underground press. Since his personality matters, choosing the right psychiatrist for a particular case can be important to the eventual outcome. Common criticisms of psychiatrists by students who had consulted them are that they were hostile or critical but in many cases it is probably the student who was projecting his own feelings.

A psychiatric opinion and treatment is probably mandatory where persistent psychotic features are present, desirable in cases of severe depression, advisable where any substantial threat of suicide exists and sensible in any case where the condition persists in spite of treatment, where the diagnosis is in doubt and where adequate time is not available to treat any psychological illness properly. Most N.H.S. psychiatrists are over-burdened hence the need for adequate psychiatric resources in the student health centre. Psychotherapy is almost unobtainable under N.H.S. arrangements.

THE PSYCHOSES

The psychoses are relatively rare in students. The main ones affecting them are manic depression, already mentioned, and schizophrenia. Both are functional psychoses meaning that no (known) physical cause is present.

The psychoses roughly corresponds to what is meant by the word insanity and imply that a qualitative change has occurred in the personality. They are distinguished from the neuroses by the fact that the patient only has limited or even no insight into his state—although a psychotic student vaguely knows he is ill—and lacks the capacity to test reality and thereby distinguish between fan-tasy and external reality. In schizophrenia other disconnections occur between thinking and feeling, between feeling and the expression of feelings, and between behaviour and intentions. The loss of grip on reality may be manifest in the sudden onset of a full-blown delusion which makes no sense but in which the patient feels that some chance observation or event is full of meaningful content. Thereafter secondary delusions may be produced in endless elaboration of the first. Hallucinations, in which voices may be heard giving instructions or a running commentary on the individual, are another example of lost reality. He may conclude that his thoughts and feelings come from outside himself as may his speech and actions. He may develop notions (delusional ideas) to explain this source of external influence and his sense of individual identity may be impaired as may the body image. He may be 'instructed' to undertake certain acts and his thoughts may suddenly cease or be subject to pressure. In conversation there is vagueness and an inability to get to the point as if the ability to mobilize thought in the desired direction has been lost. Concentration becomes difficult, thought less abstract and judgement impaired. Loss of finer feelings for others and an incongruity between thought and feeling can lead to inappropriate emotional reactions such as anger at minor frustrations and a sense of difference and separateness from others. General withdrawal may result. making it difficult to establish real contact. The emotional state may vary rapidly. Willpower may be lost, work left undone and may be replaced by philosophical, religious or sexual speculations of a fundamental kind. Instinctive impulses may break through and reveal themselves in sexual behaviour or perversions. The patient may appear childish showing rage, terror, giggling and silly behaviour, such as grimacing, rocking, putting dangerous things in the mouth and so on. Like a child he may refer to himself by name instead of 'I'.

The onset of symptoms may be fairly acute or gradual. Some disturbance such as an illness or an emotional upset may usher in the sudden changes in personality involved. The upset may at first appear to be an ordinary and acceptable adolescent response to academic stress or competition but its persistence and progress serves to alert suspicion. In one pattern the erstwhile clever school boy who compensated for social inadequacy with academic excellence becomes anxious in the face of stiffer competition and decompensates into schizophrenia. In cases of insidious onset too the presentation may initially seem like part of the variations encountered in adolescents but the patient lacks the usual resilience and the symptoms do not pass. In other cases the deterioration which occurs may seem to be no more than a worsening of certain traits of the previous personality which may have been shy, uninvolved, isolated and withdrawn, callous and indifferent to the feelings of others, over-suspicious, resentful and jealous or eccentric and bigoted. These traits, particularly the first, are aspects of the so-called schizoid personality and are possibly the product of early experiences in life. Such personalities do not necessarily lead to schizophrenia.

The picture is thus very varied and the schizophrenic student may come to notice in such a way that some other diagnosis or explanation seems to be suggested. Thus he may appear to have become lazy and be staying in bed all day, or to be over-taxed with a decline in academic performance and perhaps failure of an exam. He may claim loss of motivation and a desire to drop out; or he may be distracted by prolonged occupation with topics irrelevant to his course or show a general want of judgement in the management of his work. He may also come to notice because of withdrawal from others, depression, or anxiety, or because of hypochondriacal beliefs often based on masturbation, feelings of depersonalization or because of obsessions. Behavioural changes such as delinquent acts, a bout of promiscuity, attempted suicide or even sudden and serious attacks on others may be the first signs as may any form of bizarre and incomprehensible behaviour. Alternatively, the start may be marked by acute and obvious disturbances of mental functioning with delusions and hallucinations.

Schizophrenia is sometimes obvious in students but often it is difficult to diagnose with certainty and in consequence labels which suggest rather than confirm the diagnosis are attached to the patient. Any student in difficulty with work, emotions, interpersonal relations, thought or maintenance of contact with reality over long periods of time combined with decidedly odd, incomprehensible, unexpected or uncharacteristic behaviour may be suffering from schizophrenia. His family history and past history may help to confirm the diagnosis but equally they might not. However, many of the symptoms partake of natural experience, at least of adolescence and studenthood, so it is the overall picture and its persistent theme which are of importance rather than individual symptoms. Preoccupation with childish or pseudo-mature matters rather than the usual problems which arise in adolescence is also suggestive of schizophrenia.

Loss of contact with reality also occurs in depression where delusions, and even hallucinations, may occur but the delusions are of unworthiness and are thought to be justified by the patient. However, loss of judgement and an inability to manage affairs effectively and prudently are also present. For this reason a depressed student, or other person, should be discouraged from taking major decisions about themselves, their affairs or their future.

Hallucinations can occur in many mental diseases and even in normal people when going to sleep or waking. Certain drugs, the widest known of which is L.S.D., cause hallucinations and the state of a person who takes them resembles a psychosis. Adverse reactions can include the induction of paranoid excitement and confusion ending in aggression or suicide.

8

Exam Strain and Work Difficulties

EFFECTIVE intellectual work demands a sense of purpose and confidence as well as the necessary motivation and mental ability. Relative freedom from excessive emotional, social or physical stresses is a necessary pre-condition for most people but either because of personality structure or because work itself is the mode in which the distress is manifest (i.e. it is a refuge) some students can tolerate large burdens of adversity and not only survive but flourish. The cultivation of suitable 'philosophical' attitudes of mind can increase the ability to function effectively in the presence of much stress provided they are not used as an excuse to avoid necessary action. They can also help in the formation of a more detached view of the troubles and unpleasantnesses with which life abounds by limiting negative attitudes towards others, reducing suspiciousness about their intentions and permitting their real motivations to be seen. These are desirable qualities in students and in all professions.

THE UNDERWORKING STUDENT

Some students have fairly long cycles (weeks at a time) of relatively harder work followed by periods of relative underwork. Even effort is impossible and this is a personality characteristic more common in males. Such students may well have difficulty where a continuous assessment system is in operation. Difficulties in relation to tutors may arise leading to anxiety and resentment on the part of the student. Sometimes the underlying picture is one of cyclothymia but often it is of an all round student with many interests and intelligence but with a dislike of prolonged attention to anything. Such people think divergently and although they may not perform as well as they could in a given subject the span of their interests make them valuable.

The immature personality and students in regressed states find work difficult unless everything is to their liking and both have a low stress tolerance as do neurasthenics. This state may progress to loss of interest and reflects the lack of interest that they feel the institution, or rather the tutors, have in them and their personal needs. Underlying resentment against parents may give a motive of passive aggression. Anxious, depressed or schizophrenic students find work very hard due to the interference with concentration and will. Students with personality disorders may seek to relieve the inner and unconscious tension with acting-out involvement in pursuits peripheral to their course or in such activities as student politics and thereby work suffers. Situational distractions such as affairs, abortions, family illness, the discovery of some new pleasure or philosophy may impair work but not for very long in normal students.

Pure idleness either doesn't exist or rarely comes to the attention of the health service. Some students may give up serious attempts at work due to disappointment with the course of defeatism but such troubles are capable of remedy. Students who lack ability but who have been over-tutored in order to fulfil entrance requirements may also be overcome with defeatism but usually they struggle on to the exams thereby earning some admiration. Such cases can look like idleness and often the student will put this forward as his own explanation since it is more acceptable to him than what he really fears which is proven inability. Miscalculation of personal capability or course content can also result in underwork.

The Overworking Student

The student who overworks is probably more common than the one who underworks but he is more difficult to detect in a culture which frowns on 'swots' and views with suspicion anyone who is too compliant to the demands of teachers. The image of effortless superiority is much preferred to the one of unremitting toil. Moreover if the hard worker should fail then he has no ready excuse to explain himself. Overwork is common in women and overseas students, obsessionals and those of a hypomanic disposition. Anxiety is a spur to work and also to overwork in which the student aims to know everything word-perfect. In such cases a period of relaxation is accompanied by panicky thoughts that work he could be doing might make all the difference between getting the first or upper second he wants or even between passing and failing.

Under and Over Achievement

Although the examination system in its various forms may be the best and most practicable method of assessing both ability and effort it has its defects. Students who welcome tests of all sorts in order to display their mastery and rate themselves have advantages and the knack of success. Usually this efficiency is based on confidence gained whilst at school and if it continues well and good. Some, however, lose their nerve on joining a group of students of approximately equal ability level. There is another type of student who has success whilst at university but fails to live up to expectations subsequently. This may be due to bad luck, personality difficulties or loss of interest but it could also be due to over-assessment by the examination system. In fact this seems to occur. The best marks are not necessarily awarded to either the most intelligent, the most able or those who work hardest. Particularly worrying are cases where there are gross and apparently inexplicable inconsistencies between one year's performance and the next in the same subject.

Under achievement is commoner and the stress of examinations is probably slightly too much for the average student and his results are therefore not an altogether accurate reflection of his ability. If the effect were equal for all it would be of no concern. A poor performance in his best subject is one indicator of a student with low stress tolerance or particular vulnerability to exam strain. He is good at it and known to be good at it but when he is put to the test under examination conditions feels that all eyes are on him and his nerve fails. In spite of the increase in anxiety that his failure engenders more often than not he performs at his predicted level on re-sitting the exam. Perhaps when he is actually confronted with the evil he has always dreaded, failure, and finds he can survive it he has learned a valuable lesson and thereafter his anxiety level is less.

Particular psychic factors can play a part in achievement. For example female biology students and student nurses display very inhibited attitudes towards sex with a greater frequency than others. Their subject satisfies their interests, the more direct components of which can be held in check and denied. Personal anxieties about sex or aggression or anything else can lead to 'blind spots' in learning about them.

Work Methods

There is no method of study which ensures automatic success but some rhythm and system needs to be established if chances are to be maximized and stresses reduced. One obvious first requirement is that a system of self-discipline be established in order that work and relaxation alternate, that all subjects receive adequate attention and that the one most liked is not excessively pursued whilst the others are neglected, that difficulties in understanding are not allowed to persist and thereby engender anxiety or even a phobia about the particular subject and that set course work be completed if not on time at least in reasonable time and not allowed to accumulate. Many students report difficulty in self-management and it is hard to give any advice on the subject except to say that it can be the easiest or one of the hardest lessons of life to learn depending on attitude and resolution. Some students will settle down with work programmes set by the tutor or therapists and after a while learn to cope by themselves. Not infrequently a subject which was dreaded and which the student avoided since he regarded himself as totally incompetent at it becomes a favourite after the application of some self-discipline. In the end the institution cannot force the student to get down to work and if he is so personally disorganized that effective effort is impossible there is little hope for him unless some primary cause accessible to treatment is present.

One essential ingredient of success is confidence and this is not only a question of familiarity with the subject but also an ability to think easily within its framework. It is good advice to try to master the basic principles early on in a course of study and then to develop fluency. It is at this stage that insight occurs making subsequent laborious learning of ill-understood and unrelated facts unnecessary. For this reason the opening chapters of a text book or the introductory lectures of a course are by far the most important. Attention to apparent inconsistencies and problems is valuable for the reduction in anxiety that their solution affords.

Learning the whole of a topic at one session is more effective than learning it in parts and active learning is more effective than passive. Thus recapitulating or reciting learned material is helpful. One 'trick' that can be used in revision is for the student to pretend that he is responsible for teaching someone else the subject and with a pencil and paper he then 'instructs' his imaginary pupil. Best of all, perhaps, is for him to gain the habit of formulating questions in his own mind as if he were the examiner. When practised properly this is a highly effective method of gaining a solid grasp on a subject and is not a sterile exercise since ideas and secondary questions arise which he can pursue thereby enlarging his interest and insight. Frequent recall facilitates remembering so practice of all types is of value.

Exam Strain

Some degree of apprehension about impending examination is both normal and helpful since it serves to alert the mind and mobilize effort. After a certain level it becomes unhelpful since it interferes with effective intellectual functioning and if it increases further emotion can render the intellect totally ineffective as panic supervenes. The term exam strain is taken here to mean the presence of a level of anxiety, or depression, induced by pending examinations, which is sufficiently severe to have impaired (rather than promoted) effort for a period longer than three days. The time qualification is necessary since ordinary levels of anxiety can rise temporarily leading to a night's lost sleep or an 'attack of nerves' but the situation is quickly brought under control by the student himself. This type of 'minor panic' can result from all manner of influences such as sudden feelings that everyone knows more than he does, that insufficient time is left for him to complete his revision, that he has forgotten everything he knows and so on. Reality soon reasserts itself. Where reactions to exams amount to prolonged panic 'exam phobia' is a more appropriate term than 'exam strain'.

Symptoms of exam strain start weeks or even months before the actual exams. In some cases they subside as the exams commence but in others they become worse. In the former case the student is either the type of person who can cope with his anxiety once action is possible, or, just before the exams start he has managed to find a more philosophical attitude (i.e. a coping mechanism) of the type which asserts he has done his best to revise, that the die is cast and that further worry is pointless. This type of student is a good examinee but the other, i.e. the type who worsens as the exams commence is severely disabled. Sometimes such cases come to notice only at the last moment or even in the middle of the examinations but there is always a history of preceding exam strain although the student may have defended himself from his fears by denial.

The symptoms of exam strain are characteristic. First there are the symptoms attributable to the anxiety itself. These typically include insomnia with daytime lassitude and evidence of bad dreams —often involving calculations or unanswerable questions—provided directly or inferred from disturbed sleep. Early morning waking with a sense of dread is common but is often followed by a return to sleep and refuge in it. The student then sleeps soundly and is so determined not to wake and face reality that he may continue in that state in spite of two or three alarms or even being pulled out of bed. Smoking and masturbation increase and the student looks strained, tense, pale, sweats excessively and usually has a tremor. The appetite is usually lost (but girls may over-eat), and weight is lost. Somatic pains, particularly of the muscles and abdomen, are common and he may present with almost any physical complaint. Visual complaints and headaches are frequent. The anxiety state is not constant but fluctuates and the peaks of anxiety may be marked by disturbances of consciousness, sudden 'breakdowns' involving crying fits, attacks of overbreathing leading to tetany (in which the arms and hands go into spasm), attacks of acute pain mimicking acute abdominal or intracranial lesions, or vomiting. These may be brought on by opening a book or notes and the delusion then strikes that he remembers none of it and has forgotten everything.

The second class of symptoms arising from exam strain concern the defences which are erected against the anxiety. Although admitting to anxiety the student may deny any connection with the exams or he may produce a substitute anxiety concerning his health, his family, his girlfriend or something trivial like the exhaust system on his motor cycle. He may even deny the anxiety and display *la belle indifférence* to the exams. He may entertain rescue fantasies of being removed from his stress by some miraculous intervention or may become pre-occupied with thoughts of leading a simple stress-free life by becoming a farmer's boy. Much time may be lost with such day dreams. He may try to avoid the stress by being diagnosed as suffering from a physical illness by a G.P. or by finding reasons why he needs another year's preparation for the exam. He may regress and turn towards his family or the doctor to shoulder the burden of his anxiety and comfort him. He may begin to behave recklessly in the hope of injury or a girl may be promiscuous in the hope of pregnancy so that a credible 'excuse' is found.

The third set of symptoms derive from work. Since the exams are the feared enemy work is also an enemy and contact with it raises anxiety. Concentration is difficult, interest hard to maintain. Seduction from work by chatter, newspapers, television, making coffee or any other reasonable diversion is welcome and evening after evening passes in this way with nothing achieved leading to a secondary increase in anxiety. Sleep may supervene when a book is faced. Work may be disorganized and chaotic, the necessary items not being to hand having been 'forgotten' or 'lost'. Course work constituting part of the exam may have been neglected so that the student is in the hopeless position of either having the time to revise or do the course work but not both. Once anxiety has reached these levels effective mental work is impossible.

In the exam room either physical or mental symptoms may predominate. Writing may be near impossible due to tremor or nose bleeding may lead to withdrawal. The student's nerve may suddenly break and he has to leave due to panic. The mind may stay stubbornly blank or directions and questions on the paper may seem meaningless no matter how hard he tries to comprehend. Sudden fear that he has forgotten something he needs to know may block the mind of all thought. He may well misread the question into a form he can answer or read only the first question, and because he can do it he may then spend nearly the whole exam proving to the examiner that he knows everything about it and thus produces irrelevant and unnecessary material.

The type of student who is most vulnerable to exam strain is one who has neurotic reasons for particularly wanting success. Thus the depressive who feels worthless and who can only earn love with achievement returns to the irrational and deep anxieties belonging to childhood and fears the examiner who represents the potentially rejecting parent. Some students will not take any form of chance on an exam paper and will only write down facts of which they feel totally sure since they fear the examiner/parent will reject them with contempt for anything less than perfect. Any testing situation in which they are measured and assessed arouses all their childhood fears again. Cases of exam strain often have a history of difficulty and even failure from the earliest selective examinations undertaken, with performance falling off in university entrance examinations. They are frequently the oldest child and more often than statistics justify have parents who are involved in teaching or medicine. In the case of male students, and sometimes girls, the father is either consciously or unconsciously regarded with awe. Careful enquiry usually reveals that excessive anxiety attends almost all situations where assessment is involved and particularly with the opposite sex. Their past history judged against their abilities is always one of under performance and under achievement in either work or some other field. Even brilliant students with exam strain display this feature.

Cases of exam strain also require medical treatment and more tutorial care than average. The only mistakes the tutor can make are to dismiss the problem, give his own personal solution or, worst of all, tell the student that he is good and that great things are expected of him. This latter course may relieve the student's anxiety temporarily but only at the cost of the tutor being incorporated as an additional parental figure with high expectations which the student feels sure he cannot meet. He therefore wishes to avoid the test thereby not losing the high opinion he enjoys. Students who have been progressing well under treatment have been made unmanageable by such remarks.

Doctors have their own regimes for treating exam strain but essential steps in management include restoration of normal trouble-free sleep, relief of anxiety/depression, some attempt to overcome apathy or lassitude combined with insight into the condition, control of work and enforcement of adequate relaxation, the establishment of practices and attitudes likely to forestall examination room breakdown, and general encouragement. Brief daily consultations interspersed with longer ones every few days for a period of about six weeks are necessary if success is to be guaranteed (in so far as the success of any medical treatment can be guaranteed). Some students occasionally demand tranquillizers from doctors and then subsequently blame the therapy for their failure. The treatment of exam strain demands a good deal of medical effort and cannot be undertaken on a casual basis. Occasionally, and especially with the exam phobias, even more effort than that indicated is required and special exam room conditions and pre-examination intravenous injections may be necessary. One (brilliant) phobic girl had, after her injection, to be taken by the hand to a solitary room and the invigilator had to stand outside the door but once she had started he had not to look in at her. In order to ensure that she did not cheat she was willing, she said, if required to submit to a full search and even take the exam naked. She also had to be allowed to comfort herself with food in the proceedings.

The student with exam strain is always in difficulty since he can't do justice to himself. It may be asked that if he is as disabled as this is there any point in allowing him to graduate since the inevitable stress he will encounter in his subsequent employment will prevent him from being reliable. In point of fact this never or almost never happens. A well treated case of exam strain whose efforts have been crowned with success is permanently improved. In nearly all cases it is possible to reduce tension but the occasional case may become worse with every exam and finally may have to abandon his course. Where some underlying psychic disorder is also present then, of course, the prognosis depends upon it.

Examination Technique

Some students seem to have little or no idea of exam room technique so it not infrequently falls to the Student Health Service to instruct them. This can be incorporated into part of the treatment of exam strain and can be put over more or less as a patter in the same manner as vital actions in emergencies are taught to members of the armed services. Anxious individuals can be taught to remain effective by semi-automatic obedience to some code of self-instruction. A part of this is to make the student fantasy the dreaded situation in advance which is useful since in a severe case of exam strain the student remains unconsciously preoccupied with the impending event whilst often banishing all thoughts of it from his conscious mind. Past encounters with the examiner in the exam room remain as isolated, awful and terrifying events which are associated with a dread he can scarcely overcome. Some of the tension can be relieved by fantasy in advance and this is combined with teaching him exam technique. Such a set of instructions usually includes :

(a) When preparing for the exam try to pick out the important points which will then serve as cues for recalling the remainder. Before embarking on a piece of revision self-test your recall of the important points and then check your accuracy. Don't panic if your initial accuracy is low—simply concentrate on the topic a bit harder.

(b) Don't try to learn new material just before the exam since its learning may disturb previously remembered material by retro-active inhibition. The short-term memory is of use in the examination situation e.g. for reproducing formulae but some time must pass before more complex material is available for recall. It needs time to incubate.

(c) If you must work the night before the exam—and some personalities must—then simply try to scan the material.

(d) Get a good night's sleep before the exams if you can but don't worry if you don't—the loss of a night or two's sleep does not impair mental efficiency unless you think it does.

(e) Try to adjust mood on the morning of exams by reflections of the type that assert that when all is said and done it is only a test, that no one can be certain of success, that if you keep your wits about you it will be possible to make an attempt at almost anything that comes up, that you only need 4 out of 10 (or whatever it may be) to pass and so on.

(f) If possible try to think about other things. Try to take pride in not getting into a 'state'.

(g) Once in the exam room read the instructions. Ask the invigilator if you don't understand.

(h) Read all the questions carefully twice. Make sure you understand what is being asked of you. Long questions are usually easiest to answer. Don't be put off any of the questions at first sight. Some very easy questions look difficult on initial inspection.

(*i*) Select the questions you will answer and divide up the time.

(*j*) Remember the examiner knows you are nervous, knows you are working against the clock, won't think you are a fool for making a few mistakes and doesn't expect you to submit an answer which will entitle you to a Nobel Prize.

(*k*) Jot down a list of the important points that come into your mind as being relevant to the question you are about to answer. Other related material will then come into the mind easily. Add it to the list. First thoughts are usually correct.

(*l*) Read the question again. Eliminate all irrelevant points.

(*m*) Subject the remainder to reasoning processes which will allow you to make deductions and elaborations to amplify your answer.

(*n*) Divide the material into a beginning, a middle and end and write it down legibly.

(*o*) If you write reams you are not answering the question. Answer the question and only the question.

(*p*) Proceed through the paper answering the required number of questions.

(*q*) Write something, if only in note form, about all the questions you are required to answer.

(*r*) Take no notice of the reactions of others to the paper. Just to your best and keep going.

(*s*) If you should panic or the mind seems not to work, turn the paper face down, sit back, breathe slowly and deeply, try to think of something totally different to the examinations. Resume work when you feel better or in five minutes.

(*t*) Remember that if you keep your nerve when answering a really difficult paper you can often perform brilliantly well. Never give up. Be prepared to make guesses and take risks rather than write nothing at all. Be prepared to make guesses and take risks if necessary anyway.

Remember, also, that whatever your objections to the examination system it is not totally unlike working life itself when problems may have to be solved rapidly in the face of a shortage of time and information. To learn how to do this satisfactorily and without strain is a real asset.

9

Drugs and Drop-Outs

SOME experience with drugs is now about as common as was under-age use of tobacco a generation and more ago. The prohibition sur-rounding drugs and parental reactions against them provide, as did tobacco, a perfect means of expressing rebellion with all the advantages of the risks of police detection and subsequent martyr-dom. Students whose fathers are in the police seem to be particularly prone to being caught on drug offences.

Whether students are more likely to have some experience of drug taking than their non-student contemporaries is very hard to say but the supposition that this is at least possible seems reason-able. Accurate statistics are very hard to come by and such informa-tion as is available could be very misleading.

Routine enquiry does not lend support to a theory that use of soft drugs leads to escalation but rather that most drug usage is by way of experiment and in the majority of cases all interest is soon lost. Drug taking is a ready means of rebelling but is usually only intermittent. In some cases the student has taken drugs with the intention of exploring his personality but the cases which cause real concern are those where drug taking has been integrated into the pattern of life. In all such instances drug addiction is not a diagnosis but only a symptom of a psychic disorder and an inner distress. It is virtually impossible to turn a physically normal, healthy, reasonably happy person into a drug addict. Most students have a praiseworthy fear of all drugs, including those prescribed by doctors, and perpetually dread that exposure might impair their intellectual faculties. In fact some cases of drug taking come to light in this way with the student asking to be examined to make sure that no such harm has occurred. Some of the adverse reactions ('bad trips') seen after taking L.S.D. are much more due to the attendant anxiety than any consequence of the drug.

With the probable exception of hashish habitual use of drugs is an indication of a student in difficulty and he needs treatment for the underlying distress rather than regimes aimed at simply breaking a bad habit.

5—SH • •

Provided a sense of reason and proportion is retained drug taking can not be regarded as a problem of any great magnitude in British universities. Over-reaction against drugs, like over-reaction against sex, invites disaster but, of course, amongst medical, pharmacy or nursing students any evidence of drug taking would cause a good deal of concern. Students who are in an anxiety state or depression are often suspected of drug taking by tutors. In nearly all such cases the fears are unfounded, the students appearance merely reflecting the severity of his condition.

The relationship between drugs and 'dropping out' is of interest if only because the majority of drop-outs take drugs. However, it is wrong to assume that drug taking leads to dropping out; both are simply symptoms of the same phenomenon. In essence the drop-out is unable to overcome the emotional and academic stresses necessary to obtain success. The student who genuinely discovers that he lacks the ability, interest or industry to succeed at a particular course is not a drop-out and usually makes a success at whatever he next tackles. The true drop-out on the other hand remains involved. He tends to consort with students and use student facilities. He often dresses like a way-out student and talks like one. He may be vaguely pursuing some ill-defined intellectual aim like writing a book—or rather collecting material for one. He likes profound intellectual or pseudo-intellectual discussion and may well be applying—or thinking of applying—to various institutions for a place 'next year'. If he obtains a job it is only a temporary one and in general he takes to nothing. After a year or two he may go on his travels. More often than not an apparently despised but hard working, affluent, middle class father gives despairing support in the background but the state welfare machinery is milked to the utmost. The true drop-out often entertains political views which entitle him, in effect, to support from others as of right and without effort on his part. Depending on his personality he may be vaguely active politically or subscribe to the hippy view of life.

Behind this rather irritating and unpromising exterior there usually lies an intelligent, sensitive and somewhat immature personality who has never plucked up the courage to grasp the nettle of life. He often has a group of friends similar to himself who discuss plans which never come to fruition and, because he feels so unworthy, he is not fully committed to any heterosexual relationship in which he may be involved. He wants and needs love and approval so entering a good relationship may work wonders.

Sometimes making friends with his father or his father's death will result in a change or he may find a job which he likes and in which he does well. He may then turn up years later as a mature student or he may manage to discover a course which he likes and then succeed. Others drift into work of a type which underemploys their abilities.

Other students who are not potential drop-outs but who are under severe strain may find the drop-out culture, with its pretence of being concerned with personal worth (drop-outs normally speak of each other in extravagant terms) rather than achievement, very attractive. Since every university has its fringe drop-out group he may flirt with them for a spell and apparently adopt their values. However, he is a pseudo-drop-out since no matter what he says his underlying attitudes indicate that he has not lost any of his motivation and ambition; he is simply relieving anxiety.

Dropping out in a general sense has always been a problem in wealthy families and now it afflicts those of the professional middle classes. Each case needs investigation and treatment based on the individual and particular features. No general advice can be given to parents but a tutor who will give the student help and support whilst realizing that the rewards, at least initially, are meagre can prevent a potential drop-out from actually doing so. Punitive attitudes and threats worsen rather than improve the situation. The student needs to see some member of the staff as his understanding friend rather than a variant of his father. No matter how infrequently he may actually see them the drop-out is poorly separated from his parents and his conversation refers to them with above average frequency. A tutor who befriends a dropping-out student must be prepared to accept the dependency which goes with the condition. Communication with the parents, with the student's consent, is sometimes beneficial and sometimes harmful.

Girls drop out less frequently than boys although a girl may drop out with her boyfriend, and resort to drugs because he does. Presumably girls are less exposed to the tensions which lie behind the male 'drop-out' and in any case if she can survive until graduation she can happily drop out into marriage and comfort herself by frequent reference to the brilliant career she renounced for her husband and children.

As mentioned earlier (page 18) some students benefit by leaving their course for a year or so, during which time they can solve maturational problems, and then 'drop in' again in an improved state of mind.

10

Approach and General Treatment

THE STUDENT CONSULTATION

Since it is necessary to obtain as much relevant information as possible if an accurate diagnosis is to be made and effective treatment provided, it follows that the first aim in a student consultation is to create an atmosphere of ease and trust in which he can feel safe to talk in a significant way about his troubles. His attitude will be coloured by his relationships with significant figures in his early life, his expectations of how a doctor or tutor will behave and by the reputation of the person he is seeing. He may be guarded, garrulous, over-respectful, fearful or friendly and due note and account should be taken of this. The approach to him should be pitched accordingly and some discussion of a neutral topic for a moment or two helps to reassure him and set the scene. Some small joke or comment which makes him smile helps and as he begins to relax and sit back the consultation proper can begin. His clothes tell something of his personality and his appearance can yield eloquent evidence about his emotional state.

Since his troubles, whether they be physical or psychological, are of great concern, which he may conceal, to him he should have full attention and if some unavoidable interruption occurs an effort should be made to pick up the conversation as if the interruption had not occurred. In an unobtrusive manner his movements, rate of perspiration, facial expression and colour should all be watched and in addition to listening to what he is actually saying his choice of words, pauses, emphasis, inconsistencies and circumlocutions should be noted since they possess significance. Delay in reply, slowness, difficulty, appropriateness of response and so on all impart information and eventually a picture emerges of what he thinks the trouble is or rather how he chooses to represent it. With a little experience it is usually easy to see significant omissions, partial truths and distorted perceptions. Even if the student is allowed, apparently, to wander, not being pressed with questions, it is remarkable how eventually the main outlines, even if unconscious, become clear with an economy of words. The difficulty presented may represent or conceal his fears and even where the matter is complicated adequate clues abound. Early questions should be simple and designed to encourage him to go where he seems to wish to go but later more complicated questions designed to establish, eliminate or elaborate the various possible diagnoses revealed are required. Any questions asked by the student should be answered directly and fully unless it is deemed unwise for him to know of possible suspicions.

It has been found possible to save both parties time by using questionnaires completed before the consultation to elicit the family and past history as well as surveying the current state of health, attitude towards work, modes of relaxation and so on. Most students have no objection to this provided the purpose and confidential nature of the questionnaire are explained. Needless to say such questionnaires should not request highly private or personal details. Very often such a questionnaire is of most use when given out at the end of the first consultation with the request that it be brought back completed for the second. Certain questions can be incorporated with the aim of opening up areas of discussion so that when the replies are discussed with him these portions emerge as part of an orderly and logical sequence in the second consultation.

In any consultation no matter how short or how apparently trivial the topic it is as well to afford the student an opportunity to discuss any other problems. What then emerges may be the main point of his request for a consultation. The five broad areas that should be routinely checked are work, accommodation, family, money and interpersonal relations. In a medical interview even if the complaint is physical some of these considerations may have a bearing on the illness or affect the treatment in some way. Complaints such as insomnia, headache, tiredness, loss of appetite are usually only the superficial symptoms of a lot of underlying distress. A complaint about sleeplessness due to noisy accommodation may conceal distress about disordered interpersonal relations which may spring from a personality disorder or may signal the start of depression or even worse. As presented to a tutor the same problem may be in the form of a request for more time to hand in course work and so on. As seen by his fellow students, who may report

the facts, he may be moody, irritable, withdrawn and inappropri-
ately aggressive. However, a similar picture could also be caused
by exam strain, worry about his girlfriend being over-due or an
adolescent identity crisis in which he is feeling bewildered about
who he is, what he is doing and why.

Ideally it should be possible after one consultation to know how
the patient feels, to see life through his particular eyes. When this
is impossible and continues to be impossible the suspicion should
arise, if not there already, that a psychosis is present and reference
to a psychiatrist is advisable. Once the stage of empathy has been
reached questions can then be phrased as statements and the
patient's own statements rephrased in a more psychological manner.
Understanding and confidence then deepens which allows therapeutic advantage to be gained. The student who earlier might
have rejected advice will now say 'What would you do if you were
me?' Although views on the point vary it is the writer's opinion
that direct requests for advice should be met with advice and not
questions about what he thinks he should do. After the advice
and reasons for it have been given other alternatives can be discussed in order that the student can arrive at his own decision. To
follow any other course is to invite the student to suppose that he
is encountering indifference and perhaps make him feel generally
doubtful. Whether advice is supplied or not the form of transaction between the doctor and the student should be in the direction of promoting the student's independence and promoting his
own understanding of himself and his situation.

THERAPY

Treatment of emotional disorders should start with the first
consultation and should aim at relieving feelings, promoting insight into the self and others, establishing a relationship with the
therapist which is then replicable in relationships outside the safety
of the consulting room and promoting optimism, hope, positive
thinking, courage and suggestions concerning good attitudes. Self-
punitive and 'neurotic' attitudes should be corrected. For example,
one student was worried because he had noticed that whilst out in
industry amongst groups of new people he 'set himself up' for
obvious jests at his expense. It was his way of showing that he was
friendly and was aimed at averting more wounding criticisms that
he feared. In fact the role had been allocated when he was small

as the youngest child of somewhat disturbed parents, and was that of the family fool. This persisted to his distress. In this case merely telling him the reason was sufficient to remove the trouble but insight, by itself, is often insufficient to produce a cure. Irrational fears should be lessened and wherever possible specific treatment should be commenced for any treatable condition present. Any sexual or psychosexual disorder detected should receive prompt and thorough treatment since these are, in a sense, emergencies in late adolescents.

More formal psychotherapy may be prescribed from a psychotherapist and this is of value where prolonged treatment or detailed supervision is necessary. If a choice of psychotherapists is available some cases, other things being equal, will do best with an analytically minded therapist and others with a behaviourist. Mono-phobias seem to do very well with the latter but occasionally patients are made worse.

Group therapy is coming into vogue in student health work but on the whole a fair summary of the situation is to say that the therapist is usually more impressed with the results than the patients although there are many exceptions. Perhaps this outcome reflects poor selection of students to join the group by many therapists or discontinuity due to vacations. It may be of value in students who are not ready for 'close psychotherapy' in individual sessions. It may also be of value in certain forms to promote the release of tension through catharsis.

Treatment with medicinal drugs is not without the dangers of attempted suicide and addiction. There are ways of meeting both dangers and provided these are observed and the drug exhibited is likely to be of assistance they should be used. Unwanted side effects, especially those affecting mental alertness, are troublesome and where this occurs administration before bed is best. On the whole adolescents do not need and will not take prolonged or large doses of drugs. The correct dose is the smallest which has the desired effect and whether because of potentiation by the placebo effect or for other reasons most students require smaller doses than adults. The adolescent's resistance to drugs should be respected, since to do otherwise is to inculcate unhealthy attitudes, and where he offers to try to manage without he should be allowed to attempt it except in certain cases such as depression, epilepsy and schizophrenia.

Part of the treatment of a student consists in assessing response to therapy. Sometimes he demonstrates clear objective signs of improvement without corresponding subjective changes. These matters and the reasons for them should be discussed and pleasure should be expressed at all progress. He has often made gains only by dint of effort, and encouragement works wonders. However, generalized reassurance is out of place with students. They are always likely to challenge statements and so good reasons should underlie all that is said by the therapist.

When dealing with emotional problems it is often a good idea to set the student tasks to achieve before the next consultation. These should never exceed his capacity and should not be contradictory to his character. Such tasks may be concerned with work, self-discipline, socializing or sexual maturation. In this way the patient can be edged towards normality and better self-management.

Although opinions on the point vary it is probably wisest to extend an invitation to return whenever he wishes to a student who has completed a course of therapy. Students who have been treated for depression should be urged to return as an emergency measure at the very first sign of any recurrence since early treatment is highly effective and the use of drugs can often be avoided.

11

The Future

WHEREAS higher or tertiary education was only a short time ago the prerogative of the wealthy or the gifted and later became the entitlement of the able and motivated it is now becoming a matter of national necessity. The need to keep as many young people as possible off the labour market reflects technological advances in production which lessen the need for the unskilled and increases the requirements for experts in all manner of fields. The need is probably for more courses and more imaginative courses in higher education.

With the expansion of polytechnics, colleges and universities a greater proportion of the young are becoming students and it seems reasonable to suppose that the national need for them will increase. Some people fear that increasing demand will mean a reduction in standards due to progressively lower ability levels having to be recruited. Some suppose this has already happened but the evidence seems to indicate that there is a progressive rise in the standards that have to be achieved in order to ensure graduation.

One way in which output could be increased at minimal cost would be to reduce student wastage. Except in cases of examination failure it is often not clear why a student has left a course since a variety of reasons may be supplied but none may be the correct one. Statistics again are not a good guide. Even examination failure with its implication of academic inadequacy says nothing about the real underlying causes. It would be a very great mistake to suppose that more than a handful of students fail because they are stupid or lazy. In the main they represent potentially good material and the fifteen per cent or so who fail in many universities are not very different from the eighty-five per cent who survive. If the student was misinformed about the course and became disenchanted with it or was a misfit then the fault must lie with the institution. To the tutor such a student may appear to be indifferent, disagreeable and lacking in ability but he is likely to be none of these things. Similarly if he was unhappy, overwhelmed or troubled by psychic or adolescent difficulties the institution may be to blame if it failed to detect and rectify his troubles. The theory that the student is there to learn and he can take it or leave it is perhaps satisfactory provided he is happy and healthy in mind and body but it is less so if he is hampered by anxiety or hindered by depression. Psychic illness receives less respect than a physical illness and yet for students most physical illness does not greatly impair the ability to work.

It is true that educational institutions should not become nurseries for the adolescent or fun-fairs of fatuous happiness but early and effective intervention can preserve him from failure. Behind any failing student, with all the consequences it has for him, there are perhaps others who failed him. Sometimes it was the Student Health Service who failed to detect more sinister

motives behind his apparently simple request for some slight
medical attention. Perhaps everybody seemed too busy to have
time to listen or perhaps at the last moment his problem seemed
too silly for him to mention and no one encouraged him to do so.
Perhaps he was unassertive and timid and was met with such
hearty and managing attitudes that he couldn't bear to mention
his real trouble for fear that it or he would be dismissed out of
hand. Perhaps he felt he was treated more like a case than a whole
person so his personal problem seemed out of place. Perhaps he
felt nervous and reacted against it with an air of aggressiveness
which might have encountered a similar response from the medical
staff and so he left feeling unable to speak. He might have been
so pre-occupied with his own problems that he was rude and un-
civil which might have been taken as an offence by an inexperienced member of the health centre staff. Perhaps he simply
felt too proud to burden anyone with his problems and so did his
best to cope but failed. For all manner of reasons he may have
refrained from seeking help or when he reached a source of help
did not ask for the support he needed. Worse still the help he
received may have been inadequate or inappropriate to him in
some way. Students, after all, commonly present complex diagnostic problems so mistakes occur. He may have started on a correct
and adequate course of therapy and then, feeling somewhat better,
abandoned it. Perhaps the acceptance and response to adequate
treatment committed him to success, by removing an 'excuse' for
failure, and because this motive, which is a common one for not
responding to therapy, was undetected he again abandoned his
course of treatment.

Student Health Services are now well esablished but everyone
who works in such services must be haunted by the thought that
some of the cases of students who fail or who fail to achieve the
standard they should, really represent failures by the health service.
Perhaps the student never contacted the service and yet the service
may still be the organization that failed him since a different image
or reputation may have made it possible for him to attend. In
general the range, scope and type of services available from the
health centre are probably under publicized amongst staff and
students. Much of the printed information which is circulated to
students about the health service looks very cold and uninformative.

A good health service for students should recover their costs
many times over in the students they save from failure or under

achievement. Moreover, they should be able to contribute something to student morale. Malcontents may desist from disruptive activities if they receive proper attention. Student Health Services should prevent most suicides and unwanted pregnancies. They should contribute something towards safety and should make the major contribution to health, including sex, education. They should be able to offer general advice to the 'management' on policies designed to promote general psychic welfare but most institutions are probably still too conservative to seek or accept such advice from their doctors except in the instance of a specific student.

Many members of the academic staff are probably still too jealous of their role as the custodians of academic standards to take an outsider's opinion and experiences into account to any serious extent, and yet the Student Health Service has the means of obtaining a unique insight into the problems of students. At an individual level co-operation between the doctor and tutor works well with mutual advantage but this is still insufficiently reflected at a higher level. As stated previously health and education are old allies and it is not hard to predict that in the future both are going to have an increasing need of each other.

Perhaps the largest, most intangible and least measurable contribution of all that the Student Health Service makes is in its contribution to the future welfare of the student in later life. This aspect of the work is in a sense a by-product of its activities but in another it is true fundamental speciality. The adolescent under stress is always treated in a manner which moves him towards healthy maturity. Increasing numbers of adolescents in higher education offer the opportunity for preventive psychiatry on a massive scale. It is to be hoped that eventually the experience of student health will be utilized in providing services for all adolescents. Adolescence is a time of relatively easy re-adjustment and such services as are available for adolescents do not lack patronage by them. Although all manner of different views are expressed about the age group the adolescent *is* a special person. Help given at this time is probably equal in effectiveness to many times greater help given later. In fact, in many cases it is possible that if the opportunity is missed no amount of subsequent effort will ever remedy the defect.

Students and adolescents in general are not far from adulthood and parenthood. They are also at the outset of their careers. To ensure that they proceed free of significant handicaps and with

all the confidence possible is one way of creating a better society.
No educational institution can fulfil this aim without the assistance
of a well developed Student Health Service.

12

Some Theoretical Considerations

IN spite of the huge volume of medical knowledge medicine has
been aptly compared to islands of light in a sea of darkness. This
is particularly true of those illnesses arising from, connected with
or which are expressed as disturbances of human feeling and
behaviour.

Simple reassurance and a few tablets may be sufficient to cure
the more trivial cases and the most serious may only respond to
physical methods of treatment and intensive drug therapy but
between these extremes lie the vast majority of cases characterized
by distress, to the patient or others, inefficiency and failure of one
sort or another. Any theory which provides a basis for comprehending the underlying and invisible causes of the condition and which
also can be utilized in treatment is of the utmost value. The fact
that the theory 'works in practice' does not necessarily validate
the theory but this is of less concern to the doctor responsible for
the case than the scientist. However, to dismiss the theory on the
grounds that it lacks 'hard, objective evidence' is also unscientific;
the furthest one can go is to suspend judgement. It is perhaps
worth remembering too that Freud and those who have continued
his work have not been armchair theoreticians but have been involved in the battle against *dis-ease*. Their theories have been the
practical formulations of practical men and women. It is probably
for this reason that the theories are not totally compatible.

TOPOGRAPHIC THEORY

Freud deduced from observation of his cases that there were topographically three systems in the psychic apparatus, namely, the unconscious, the preconscious and the conscious. The first is inaccessible to consciousness, non-verbal, instinctual, infantile and concerned with pleasure and the wish for it. It contains those fantasies and experiences of childhood and adolescence which are unacceptable to the preconscious mind and have therefore been repressed by it. This is done by the operation of a censor in the preconscious which relaxes a little during sleep thereby permitting some of the material in the unconscious to be perceived in dreams. When awake the preconscious delays the discharge of instinctual energy in accordance with the dictates of logic, reality, conscience and so on. Material in the preconscious mind can be easily made conscious and the conscious mind pays selective attention to events in the outer world and to thoughts and feelings in the preconscious but is unaware of the unconscious.

Symptoms arise when the repressed material in the unconscious becomes too strong to be contained or when the censor is enfeebled. Neurotic or psychotic symptoms are then produced. Neurotic anxiety thus results from a failure in repression. If a sexual act or wish, for example, is accompanied by anxiety then repression has taken place. However, the anti-instinctual forces are also often unconscious and this is not in accord with the function of the preconscious. Freud therefore introduced another theory which seemed to offer a better explanation of the phenomena displayed by the patients he treated when they were in situations of conflict over an instinctual drive.

STRUCTURAL THEORY

The new theory asserted that the mind consists of two structures, namely the id and the ego. The moral functions of the ego were subdivided off into the superego. The id contains the instinctual drives which were said to be basically aggressive and libidinal. The ego gradually develops as the nervous system of the child evolves permitting it to perceive and exploit opportunities for instinctual gratification. Ego development is also affected by the child's object relations i.e. his experiences arising from contact with persons in his environment. If the experiences both afford gratification and impose frustrations in reasonable proportions the object relations are good and assist in the process of identification (see later). The ego is concerned with consciousness, sense perception, voluntary movement, rational thought, memory, language, defence mechanisms, synthesis and reality-testing in which inner fantasies are distinguished from outer facts. The superego is concerned with moral commands and prohibitions and, with ideal aspirations. It forms first around the prohibitions of the parents and it is harsh and cruel. The ego-ideal does not emerge in final form until adolescence when it is a narcissistic regard for self and represents 'how I am, intend or wish to be'. Offending the superego leads to feelings of guilt, remorse and a desire for punishment but upsets of the ego-ideal lead to shame. Like the rest of the ego some elements in the superego are accessible to consciousness and some are not but the id is largely denied such access.

During childhood every child discovers from experience that certain events, such as his mother leaving him or parental displeasure with him, are associated with feelings of unpleasure and his ego responds with feelings of anxiety. Thus when a wish comes into his mind which will earn disapproval he becomes anxious and so opposes the wish in order to avoid unpleasure. A conflict then develops between the ego and the id. The ego develops the means to oppose the wishes and these are called the defences. They may be successful and permanently block the wish or unsuccessful and produce neurotic symptoms. All actions, fantasies, dreams and symptoms are thus a compromise between instinctual forces, moral prohibitions, defences and external reality.

PSYCHO-ECONOMICS

Psychological work such as thinking, emoting or remembering requires psychic energy. The instincts provide the energy so its source is the id. The id invests energy in images of objects (i.e. hallucinations) or in action on objects to satisfy a need. The energy is easily displaceable and objects are easily confused which is irrational. The id cannot distinguish between external objects and their images but as a child grows up it begins to form accurate mental representations of the real world and so the ego starts to develop thereby establishing contact with reality along with rational thought. Normally, in adults, the ego utilizes most of the id energy, except in sleep when the hallucinatory wish-fulfilment type of thinking which belongs to infancy returns. The ego often has to use energy to oppose the demands of the id for immediate gratification and the id may then have to be satisfied with a fantasy instead of action but it may break through the restraints of the counter-forces leading to impulsive behaviour.

The interplay between the forces promoting and preventing action is a dynamic state. Thus, the counter-forces of an early adolescent may be unable to withstand the increases in instinctual tension occurring at that time and neuroses often start then. The diversion of a great deal of energy to the solution of an inner problem gives rise to feelings of tiredness although little or no physical work may have been undertaken.

Libido Theory

Psychoanalytic theory is called dynamic because, in contrast to learning theory which is concerned only with the effects of learning from experience, it, and related theories, explain behaviour in terms of innate instinctual developmental processes. An instinct is the psychic representative of a somatic need and has the aim of removing the instinctual need with the assistance of an object in the outer world.

The libido is mental energy and in the new-born child it is largely invested in the mouth through which the child obtains sensory satisfaction. Later primacy passes to the anus and then to the phallus. Each stage is synchronized with ego development. These stages are pre-oedipal and auto-sexual.

The oedipal story—which turns so many people against Freud—seems to be entirely plausible and supportable with clinical evidence. In essence it seems simple and indeed obvious that once the ego has begun to develop and the environment contains identifiable people the small child loves and wishes to be loved particularly by its opposite sex parent. The oedipal child loves with the totality of its being which includes its sexuality but this is not to say that at the time the child knows, seeks or understands adult sexual practices. Why a child should orientate itself particularly to its opposite sex parent is not known. It may be instinctive or depend on the different ways in which we as parents treat our own and the opposite sex. Even if it is an instinct it can be overruled by experience and a father who, for example, rejects his daughter must harm her future capacity to relate to men. To deny this amounts to denying that experience has significance and this is manifest nonsense. How the child resolves the anxieties and frustrations which the oedipal situation imposes can be nothing but fateful for the individual's future emotional and sexual life with the opposite sex in particular and his own personality development in general. Faulty solutions create faulty adults unless corrected. The superego seems to develop from an early age but grows rapidly as the oedipal problem is solved.

IDENTIFICATION AND IDENTITY

Thereafter the child is likely to identify more strongly with the same sex parent and aims to be like them or some aspect of them. He may also increasingly identify with other figures. Sometimes identification is based on perceived similarities to the self and is known as narcissistic. Where carried too far a man who loves himself exclusively may extend his love to other males (identifies with them) and this may be one cause of homosexuality. Sometimes it is based on behaving the same way as someone else in order to obtain the desired success they have. For example, an early adolescent girl will want to dress in the same manner as her older sister in order to obtain boyfriends as she does. Another method of identification is used by children who have been rejected, or who feel they have been rejected, by their parents (see page 62). They try to live up to what they think the parents want of them. Yet another method is to behave in accordance with (identification with) the precepts of parents or others of significance who will inflict punishment for a breach of behaviour. All this serves to mould the personality.

In adolescence identity formation begins (according to Erikson) by a process of repudiation or acceptance of different portions of earlier identifications and this combined with the experimentation permitted in the psychosocial moratorium of adolescence allows him to find his own niche or identity. However, identity crises occur as old battles are refought in order to restore a sameness and continuity between the roles and skills acquired in childhood and the prospective ones which are to develop in adulthood. The identity crisis is accompanied by role diffusion in which the adolescent becomes unpredictable, renounces commitment and experiments with danger, deviance and fantasies normally repressed in adults (see page 32). If carried too far a state of acute identity diffusion which borders on schizophrenia may result in which the adolescent may negatively identify with (i.e. be the opposite of) the norms of his family and community, lose the ability to concentrate and the ability for intimacy. Some discussion in student health revolves round the concept of 'normal' identity crises i.e. whether they should be diagnosed and accepted as a part of normal adolescence. There are dangers in accepting identity crises as transient but normal phenomena since any pathological distress lying behind the adolescent's troubles may be missed, and this is the opportunity to relieve them. Even transient disorders may be product of the interaction between the contemporary situation and an underlying disability which is not normally apparent; indeed this is the basis of neurotic reactions in general. However, normal adolescent adjustment reactions do occur, and could be regarded as identity crises.

The identity must contain within it good attitudes towards work, achievement and occupational role if success as a student is to be assured. It is probably the lack of these combined with a lack of early educational influences in the home which excludes an undue proportion of unskilled and semi-skilled workers' children from higher education. The identity must also contain attitudes towards the opposite sex based on strong identifications with a figure of one's own sex if love and sex needs are to find total fulfilment.

THE DEFENCES

The ego has a very hard life and, as Freud pointed out, we are always saying so. Ideally the ego should cope directly with all difficulties whether they arise from the instincts, conscience or reality but in practice it is not always strong enough to achieve this and so it develops mechanisms, called defences, for warding off unpleasant feelings such as anxiety and guilt without directly facing up to them. In this way harmony is maintained between the id, superego and reality. Of these defences **repression** the commonest. Painful memories or urges are pushed down into the unconscious and for all conscious purposes cease to exist. Matters pertaining to sex are often repressed in our culture.

The facility with which repression can occur is astounding. For example, a very distressed final year student complained of inability to eat, work and sleep. She felt perpetually anxious and depressed (hating herself), couldn't face people and burst into tears on the slightest provocation. She was normally a fairly placid girl free of any serious personality difficulties who could speak openly about herself. She has no conscious idea of the cause of her distress but suggested and finally stated, with some supporting reasons, that it must be due to an essay that was giving her difficulty. On investigation this was thought to be an insufficient cause. It was obvious that she was trying to bring about the *displacement* of her anxiety from its real source to a more acceptable one. In response to a set routine of questioning designed to investigate every aspect of the contemporary situation it slowly emerged that she had had intercourse for the first time two nights earlier.

Her manifest agitation greatly increased as the subject was approached but she began to try to lead the conversation in other directions and responded to simple straight forward questions as if she could not comprehend their import. This was in sharp contrast with her earlier openness. In this she was showing *resistance* which was totally unconscious on her part.

When it became obvious what had happened and the matter was put to her directly she at first launched on a *denial* that the event had occurred but then rapidly shifted to a fresh defence (against herself and her behaviour) which asserted that even if it had occurred then it wasn't of much significance. She said that sex wasn't all that important to her, that she had long fantasied the event in anticipation and its actuality could not therefore upset her much, that she had in any case often been half way there before etc., etc. She put forward these reasons or *rationalizations* in the form of a series of *intellectualizations* with the unconscious aim of depriving what she had done of the awful significance that she all too obviously but unconsciously attributed to it herself. Her superego was outraged and in the face of its attack she had no alternative but to resort to *repression* of the memory and was in a state of **regression** equivalent to that of a frightened little girl. This defence showed that her earlier attempt in the consultation to regard the act in **isolation** from the attendant guilt feelings (which she had repressed) had failed.

Earlier in adolescence she had thought herself unattractive and this combined with her hostility to her sexuality had compelled her to adopt a series of **sublimations** of repressed sexual instincts, the chief of which was work from which she derived deep satisfaction. However, this was still insufficient and she had therefore formed a number of **reactions** against her residual sexual interests by making a big point of being uninterested in boys but interested in religion and babies. She was also prudish. By late adolescence this defence had weakened leaving her somewhat interested in sex and boys. However, she had been through a stage in which she had suffered from the **projection** of her own partly conscious but mainly unconscious deep sexual desires on to the boys she met and she had been afraid of them because she felt that given any chance at all they would have forced her to have intercourse. In fact she had chosen a very inhibited boy for her friend. It was only by choosing such a boy that her superego had allowed her to have a boyfriend at all.

During her association with him she had sought treatment for a number of physical complaints including headaches and genital pains. No cause was found for these and they had been assumed to be due to the *conversion* of her anxieties about the relationship into symptoms thereby ensuring psychic comfort. However, her complaints had often made 'petting' impossible. In retrospect she thought she had been much keener on physical experience than he but at the time she had felt that anything she had done she had undertaken only to please him and not herself. In this way, she agreed, she had practised *dissociation* in order to protect herself from the guilt she would have otherwise experienced had she consciously accepted that she yearned for sexual stimulation.

Finally, she faced up to what she had done and began to talk about her experience in an adult way. She had been trying to achieve *withdrawal* from the situation by *avoiding* her boyfriend in order to maintain her *repression* but had also entertained conflicting desires to see him and repeat the act. These thoughts too she had repressed and her first account of herself had omitted all reference to him. Her anxiety and depression disappeared and she started to take practical steps to deal with her changed situation. She began to admit to herself the pleasure she had experienced and a month or two later she had decided that such an inhibited boyfriend was not a good marriage prospect unless he improved. She was becoming doubtful about their rather vague future plans in that direction. In *compensation* for her feelings of unattractiveness she improved her appearance and became much more involved with men generally.

Any of the defences mentioned could have become entrenched

and prohibited her from making any further progress but at another level the defences can be seen as a series of self-deceptions by means of which she finally obtained the goal she sought. Any direct seeking of the goal without the intervention of her defences would have been utterly impossible. In this sense they were more mental mechanisms to shield her from discomfort rather than fixed defences. During her period of distress she had had a feeling of impending catastrophe combined with—or induced by—a desire for punishment in atonement for the sin she had committed. This occurs not uncommonly in students and is a form of **undoing** the wrong they feel they have done.

The defences set in bold italics are those 'officially' accepted (A. Freud) by psychoanalysts. To them are added three more. **Turning against self** occurs, for example, in obsessional neurosis where the desire to torture is turned into self-torture. **Reversal** depends upon the capability of instincts to be reversed. Thus sadism, which is active, may be turned into the passive state of masochism thereby reducing anxiety. **Introjection** means the taking into the mind a representation of an external object, such as the mother or lover. In this way the anxiety which arises when separation from the object occurs can be diminished.

Defences distort reality. Therefore extensive and permanent reliance on them as in the psychoses and personality disorders is a serious matter but they are also used in ordinary everyday life in 'normal' people when they serve adaptive purposes. Indeed, they are part of a 'normal' personality and anyone devoid of defences would be mad. The need to utilize them arises from unwelcome thoughts and emotions which are unacceptable to the self. They are therefore commonly seen in adolescents and students who use them to reduce the stress to which they are subject. The presence of a defence shows that anxiety and distress are also present.

Coping Mechanisms

The defences function in the unconscious mind but at a more conscious level, coping mechanisms are used to relieve tension. They make the stress to be endured tolerable to the individual. Examples have been mentioned earlier and include refuge in sleep or in daydreams which give the dreamer what he feels he most needs to solve his difficulty. Increases in food consumption or masturbation before exams are more the result of a need for self-comfort than instinctual satisfaction. Tension may be worked off by violent exercise, alcoholic excess, compulsive talking or a good row. A student who feels sad and defeated by some social reverse may play 'mood' records to himself for hours and so finally relieve his distress. Seeing 'the bright side' or 'the funny side' are other examples of coping mechanisms. If relied on permanently the mechanisms become evasions of reality and are fatuous but an adequate and versatile collection of such mechanisms is of the utmost value to a student.

RESPONSE TO STRESS

Stress is anything which causes distress whether the origin be internal or external or whether the effects be physical or psychical. The response can be adaptive or maladaptive. Psychic stress, and particularly that concerned with instinctual needs and object relations, seem to provoke one or more of the following responses in those who maladapt to it.

(a) Physical symptoms, e.g. blushing, fainting, susceptibility to disease.
(b) Psychosomatic symptoms.
(c) Psychological symptoms
        (i) anxiety
        (ii) depression
(d) Psychiatric disorders
        (i) personality disorders
        (ii) behavioural disorders
        (iii) neuroses
        (iv) psychoses

Provided their use is not excessive the avoidance of stress provoking situations, evasions, retreat, self-deceptions, defences, coping mechanisms, self-indulgence, impulsive behaviour, verbalization (including catharsis), alterations in existing interpersonal relations or establishing new ones are all examples of 'normal' ways for coping with the stress of life.

A 'breakdown' is a form of evasion of an extreme kind. It is a lay rather than a medical concept and implies a state, not amounting to madness, in which normal functioning is impossible and care in hospital may be necessary. Many of the students who ask to see a psychiatrist are contemplating having a breakdown and complaints that they feel they are on the verge of a breakdown are commonplace amongst students. Having a breakdown can be disastrous academically and raises questions about whether the student has the emotional fortitude to complete his course. In cases where it seems he has not, or where it seems unlikely that treatment will be of sufficient help or where the real underlying cause is an irremedial loss of motivation then abandoning the course is probably in his best long term interests. However, this is not a situation where quick judgements are necessarily justified. Giving the student maximum clinical and tutorial care combined with strong general support can work wonders even in cases which look hopeless at first sight. Probably all Student Health Services receive letters from long departed ex-students who were in this situation but survived and then attribute all their subsequent success to the treatment they received.

The Nature of Neurosis

Further to what has been previously said (pages 48 and 106) it is apparent that the neuroses appear to the patient as unintelligible changes in feeling i.e. as anxiety or depression, in thoughts i.e. as obsessions or compulsions, in sensations or functions as in hysteria or in fear as in phobias. Irrational ways of dealing with inner impulses and outer reality are substituted for normal ones and the effect may be either to disturb the whole character of the individual or only to lead to the production of symptoms. The patient, unlike the psychotic, can distinguish reality and knows he is ill.

Neurotic phenomena are viewed as involuntary emergency discharges of psychic energy which supplant normal ones due to an insufficiency of normal control. This comes about either by there being too much excitement for the apparatus to master which is traumatic or by the complete or partial blockage of discharge, due to past causes in the personality and life-experience, which has the effect of allowing normal excitations to operate like traumatic ones. The latter state is the cause of the psychoneuroses in which there is a conflict between the id and the defences of the ego resulting in tension which is discharged in a distorted fashion as a neurotic symptom without the consent of the ego and is therefore experienced as alien.

The student who had been blown up by a bomb (page 45) was suffering from a traumatic neurosis. The symptoms have the effect of allowing the patient to assimilate and work through the shock of the event. Occasionally such a neurosis turns into a psychoneurosis i.e. hysteria, obsessions or phobias. Less dramatic traumata than this occur in childhood when the ego is weak and has difficulty in controlling anxiety. Such matters as physical violence, separation from parents, disturbed family relationships and sexual assaults are examples as are failures to deal successfully with oedipal anxiety and these result later, as stated above, in neurosis.

An anxiety neurosis is any neurosis of which anxiety is a marked feature.

THE NATURE OF PSYCHOSIS

Traumata are also thought to be important in the psychoses. The individual regresses to an earlier developmental stage than the neurotic and the mind functions as in infancy or dreams. Hallucinations and delusions are therefore common and the patient withdraws interest from the real world thereby becoming incapable of distinguishing reality from fantasy. The ego's ability to synthesize and integrate the functions of the id, superego and reality is impaired so everything seems confused to the patient. Freud thought that the withdrawn interest was invested in either the self or the body leading to megalomania or hypochrondriasis respectively. They were thus seen by him as narcissistic disorders.

MATURITY

It will be obvious by now that one of the main difficulties arising in the psychological treatment of students is to decide whether the problems arising are attributable to immaturity or the presence of pathology. The distinction is of enormous importance since to confuse the two is to do the patient harm.

Faults in emotional development create emotional problems which then block or deviate development. Resolution of the difficulty allows maturation to proceed but the delay may have caused permanent harm since it seems that certain tasks have to be achieved in certain critical stages. Thus in some cases the doctor or therapist has to accept and persuade the patient to accept a degree of malfunction in just the same manner as he may have to accept, for example, an orthopaedic disability.

Against this background it is useful to list the characteristics of maturity by way of further amplification of those already given (pages 47 to 51). These have been formulated by Saul.

(a) A capacity to live independently of the parental organism. Failures here include dependent personality disorders, neuroses, neurotic behaviour and those whose dependence/independence conflicts produce symptoms.

(b) Capacity for responsibility and productivity. Those who were deprived or over-indulged emotionally cling too much to getting and give too little.

(c) A relative freedom from inferiority feelings, egotism and competitiveness. Feelings of inferiority and a great desire to compete belong to childhood and therefore remain to some extent in adults. (The id never learns and never grows up.) When present excessively they cause anxiety and guilt which reduces the capacity to enjoy work and love.

(d) Socialization and domestication. This is a function of the superego which should not only be negative but should also further innate tendencies towards co-operation. Too little or too lax training in childhood results in an impulse-ridden adult; too much, too early or too harsh training results in inhibited adults and inconsistent training in indecisive ones.

(e) Capacity for love and productivity both social and sexual. After the oedipal stage of libidinal development there is said to follow a stage of latency in which instinctual interests are lessened thereby freeing the child to develop all manner of talents. With puberty the genital stage arises and affords a new capacity for object interest outside oneself. This provides a powerful and constant impetus towards maturity. Too much severe restraint in childhood prevents sexual maturity and satisfaction, too little may make sex a matter for personal pleasure rather than a basis for a proper relationship.

(f) Gentleness. Frustration and fear arouse fight or flight reactions and are normal but chronic aggressiveness is derived from unresolved emotional problems of childhood. Revenge for mistreatment as a child and feelings of weakness from being driven into submissiveness result in later anger, hate, cruelty and belligerency. This is displaced on to others (e.g. from mother to wife) or even on to the individual himself as in the neuroses or in personal mismanagement. If the individual is strong and not weak he can be gentle.

(*g*) A firm sense of reality. The schizoid personality remains detached, the rejected depressive, the over-protected unduly
optimistic and the guilty threatened (i.e. paranoid).

(*h*) Flexibility and adaptability. Where childhood problems have
been solved by permanent and fixed changes in the personality (i.e. a personality disorder) the capacity for flexible
personality adaptations is lost.

Maturity gives the individual pleasure from the exercise of his
adult powers in addition to continuing to satisfy, within reason,
needs which first arose in infancy.

Further Reading

STUDENT HEALTH

Emotional Problems of the Student, G. B. Blaine and C. C. McArthur (Butterworths 2nd ed. 1971)

Psychiatry, Education and the Young Adult, D. L. Farnsworth, (Charles Thomas 1966)

A Handbook on British Student Health Services, N. Malleson (Pitman Medical Publishing Co. 1965)

Student Casualties, A. Ryle (Penguin Press 1969)

Tutors and their Students, M. Sim (Livingstone 2nd ed. 1970)

STUDENTS

University Student Performance, D. McCracken (British Student Health Association 1969)

Students Away from Home, A. H. B. Ingleby (National Marriage Guidance Council 1970)

The Campus War, J. Searle (Pelican 1972)

Enquiry into Student Progress, University Grants Committee (H.M.S.O. 1968)

Educational Survey, J. Wankowski (University of Birmingham 1970)

ADOLESCENCE

On Adolescence, P. Blos (Free Press 1962)

Stress in Youth, M. Capes, E. Gould and M. Townsend (Oxford University Press 1971)

Adolescence, G. Caplan and S. Lebovici (eds.) (Basic Books 1969)

The Severely Disturbed Adolescent, W. M. Easson (International Universities Press 1969)

Childhood and Society, E. H. Erikson (Pelican 1965)

The Adolescent in Psychotherapy, D. J. Holmes (Little, Brown & Co., 1964)

Modern Perspectives in Adolescent Psychiatry, J. G. Howells (ed.) (Oliver & Boyd 1971)

Adolescents, S. Lorand and H. I. Schneer (Harper & Row 1961)

The Psychiatric Dilemma of Adolescence, J. F. Masterton (Little, Brown & Co. 1967)

The Fragile Alliance, J. E. Meeks (Williams & Wilkins 1971)

Child Development and Personality, P. H. Mussen, J. J. Conger and J. Kagan (Harper International 3rd ed. 1969)

Psychological Disturbance in Adolescence, I. B. Weiner (John Wiley 1970)

Health Problems of Adolescence, W.H.O. Technical Report No. 308 (1965)

Mental Health of Adolescents and Young Persons, W.H.O. Public Health Paper No. 41 (1971)

GENERAL PSYCHIATRY AND MEDICAL PSYCHOLOGY

Psychiatry, E. W. Anderson and W. H. Trethowan (Bailliere, Tindall & Cassell 2nd ed. 1967)

American Handbook of Psychiatry, Vol 3, S. Arieti (ed), (Basic Books 1966)

Depression, A. T. Beck (Staples Press 1967)

The Psychotic, A. Crowcroft (Pelican 1971)

Psychological Medicine, D. Curran, M. Partridge and P. Storey (Churchill Livingstone 7th ed. 1972)

Fears and Phobias, I. M. Marks (Heinemann 1967)

Psychology in Relation to Medicine, R. M. Mowbray and Roger T. Ferguson (Churchill Livingstone 3rd ed. 1970)

Short Textbook of Psychiatry, W. L. Linford Rees (English Universities Press 1970)

Anxiety and Neurosis, C. Rycroft (Pelican 1971)

Emotional Maturity, J. Saul (Lippincott 3rd ed. 1971)

Clinical Psychiatry, E. Slater, M. Roth (Bailliere, Tindall & Cassell 3rd ed. 1970)

Suicide and Attempted Suicide, E. Stengel (Pelican 1964)

Prevention of Suicide, W.H.O. Public Health Papers No. 35 (1968)

PSYCHOANALYSIS

Psychoanalytic Concepts and the Structural Theory, J. A. Arlow and C. Brenner (International Universities Press 1964)

Thrills and Regressions, M. Balint (Hogarth Press 1959)
Freud and the Post-Freudians, J. A. C. Brown (Pelican 1966)
The Psychoanalytic Theory of Neurosis, O. Fenichel (Routledge
& Kegan Paul, reprinted 1971)
The Ego and the Mechanisms of Defence, A. Freud (Hogarth
Press 1951)
Complete Psychological Works of Sigmund Freud, S. Freud
(Hogarth Press 1951)
A Primer of Freudian Psychology, C. S. Hall (Mentor Books 1954)
New Directions in Psychoanalysis, M. Klein (ed.) (Social Science
Paperbacks 1971)
Reconstructions in Psychoanalysis, M. T. McGuire (Meredith
Corporation 1971)
Introduction to the Psychoanalytic Theory of the Libido, R. Sterba
(Robert Brunner 3rd ed. 1968)
Freud, R. Woleheim (Fontana 1971)

DEFINITIONS

A Dictionary of Psychology, J. Drever (Penguin, reprinted 1972)
*A Comprehensive Dictionary of Psychological and Psychoanalytical
Terms,* H. B. English and A. C. English (Longman reprinted
1970)
A Critical Dictionary of Psychoanalysis, C. Rycroft (Nelson 1968)

SEX AND RELATIONSHIPS

Textbook of Psychosexual Disorders, C. Allen (Oxford University
Press 1962)
Husbands and Wives, R. O. Blood, Jr. and D. M. Wolfe (Collier
Macmillan 1960)
Fundamentals of Sex, P. Cauthery (Illustrated by M. Cole)
(Allens 1971)
Sexual Discord in Marriage, M. Courtenay (Tavistock 1968)
Marital Tensions, H. V. Dicks (Routledge & Kegan Paul 1967)
Sexual Function and Dysfunction, P. J. Fink and O. Hammett
Van Buren (F. A. Davis 1969)
Disorders of Sexual Potency in the Male, J. Johnson (Pergamon
1968)
Development of Sex Difference, E. Maccoby (ed.) (Tavistock 1968)

Dynamics of Deviant Sexuality, J. H. Masserman (ed.) (Grune & Stratton 1969)

The Sexual Behaviour of Young People, M. Schofield (Longman 1965)

Sexual Deviation, A. Storr (Pelican 1964)

Sex and its Problems, W. Thomson (ed.) (Livingstone 1968)

Counselling, Ethel Venables (The National Marriage Guidance Council 1971)

Sexual Problems, C. W. Wahl (Free Press 1967)

Index